FROM BOTH SIDES NOW

Memories of an Austro-Hungarian Fighter and POW in World War I Italy

Edited by Ingrid Cranfield

FROM BOTH SIDES NOW
Copyright © Ingrid Cranfield, 2021

All Rights Reserved

No part of this book may be reproduced in any form, by photocopying or by any electronic or mechanical means, including information storage or retrieval systems, without permission in writing from both the copyright owner and the publisher of this book.

ISBN 978-1-7398219-0-6

First Published December 2021
Published by Ingrid Cranfield

FROM BOTH SIDES NOW

Contents

The Genesis of this Book 1

Acknowledgements 5

Severin Breier: A Biography 9

The Beginning of WW1 56

DIARY 1 58

DIARY 2 92

DIARY 3 148

Place Names 156

*In admiring and loving memory of Severin Breier (Briar),
a hero in war and in peacetime*

"To my dearly beloved Mama from your loyal son Severin.
Jägerndorf [Krnov, Czech Republic], 4/II/1917"

1981

The Genesis of this Book

My father, Severin Briar (formerly Breier), died in October 1981 on holiday in northern Italy. His wife, my mother Annette, having tried unsuccessfully to live without him, died in June 1985, also on a trip abroad, in this case to then East Germany. Both had been living in the UK. When Annette died, the archives, mementoes, photos and other memorabilia from both of them passed down to their daughters, Beatrice and me.

Apart from translating the first of Severin's war diaries (Diary 1), which he himself had transcribed from Gabelsberger German shorthand in 1979, two years before he died, and investigating some of the papers and records of Annette's family, neither Beatrice nor I did much with this inheritance until now.

In 2014, the London Borough of Enfield staged an exhibition to mark the start of WWI. I delved into my archives and was able to find some objects and documents from Severin's war experience, and they were placed in their own individual exhibit case, representing 'the other side'. Severin fought on the side of the Austro-Hungarians against the British. However, it goes without saying that the experience of an 18-year-old in a war is much the same as that of any other 18-year-old in a war, whichever side they are fighting on.

The editor with the exhibit case displaying items from Severin's collection of memorabilia from WWI. At the time, I was Deputy Mayor of the London Borough of Enfield.

This was one reminder that the archives are still in my possession. In 2018, there were celebrations and events around the world to mark the end of WWI. At that time, I remembered the second of Severin's war diaries (Diary 2), which I had asked a Viennese colleague to transcribe 30 years earlier but which he had found too difficult a task. I then decided that I had a duty to get the second diary transcribed, translated and, if possible, published. It took a few months of searching on the internet and being referred from one person to another before I found Dr. Jascha-Alexander Koch, a stenography specialist based in Langen, near Frankfurt, Germany. I scanned the pages of the diary and sent them to Jascha, who was able electronically to sharpen the images and agreed to do the transcription. It took the best part of two years for the work to be finished, owing to Jascha's other commitments and challenges. I also asked Jascha to transcribe the last few pages of Severin's 1981 diary (Diary 3), knowing that it would contain a reference to the last excursion Severin undertook, which was emotionally linked with his experience as a POW in Mola di Bari, Italy, in 1918-19.

- Diary 1 covers 1 August 1917 to 14 October 1917. This includes Severin's participation in the 11th Battle of Isonzo.

- Diary 2 covers September 1918 to September 1919. This includes Severin's participation in the battles of the Val di Frenzela and his incarceration as a prisoner of war in Mola di Bari.
- Diary 3 covers a week in October 1981. This refers to Severin's last holiday in the Merano region of northern Italy.

Having translated the diaries into English, I translated a passage from *Der Kleine Beckmann*, a *Whitaker's Almanack*-type encyclopaedia and dictionary, that described the battlefield terrain and the actions that took place during the 11th Battle of Isonzo, in which Severin took part (Diary 1).

As one thing led to another, I dug out boxes of memorabilia relating to Severin's war and POW experiences. In them I found the medal he won for bravery, a newsletter published in the POW camp, letters and postcards, ID cards and many other documents and items. They had been kept for a reason, and the reason was not simply that someone should periodically take them out of the boxes and look at them before putting them back again, but that they should be processed, understood, disseminated and appreciated as revealing not only family and personal history but also the history of the time, as seen from Severin's wartime point of view.

Photos and other illustrations of Severin's life before and after the war have also been assembled here.

All the material in German has been translated into English by me. There are gaps in the transcription and hence in the translation, as the second diary was written in pencil, which has faded quite drastically in places over the last 100 years. Where there were so many gaps that it was impossible to gauge the meaning, I have sometimes simply edited out a small passage. Remaining gaps are mostly marked with [...]. It was not possible to find exact equivalents for some of the terms, notably military titles and names of units; however, the nearest terms are presented here. Moreover, where it was mainly possible to decipher ordinary words written in shorthand, personal names often posed a challenge, since in shorthand they were rendered phonetically. Thus, for example, it was almost impossible to know whether Severin was referring to someone called Kriesch, Kritsch, Krietsch or Krisch, and some guesswork and knowledge of more common names were employed.

Further, a few of the documents reproduced or referred to here were written in the old German script and were also faded or damaged. Again, I was able to part-decipher these, or at least to get the gist of them, but complete accuracy was not possible.

Any faults in the translations are entirely mine.

Thus, what started out as a limited exercise, involving nothing more than transcribing and translating Diary 2, became a book.

The structure of the book is essentially that of main roads and side roads. The three diaries form the main roads; the other materials, which refer to or illustrate the content of the diaries, represent the side roads.

The title, *From Both Sides Now*, represents the fact that war brings the same horrors, terrors, sorrows and triumphs to anyone engaged in it, and that what happened over a hundred years ago is as relevant today as it was significant then.

Ingrid Cranfield
Editor
2021

Acknowledgements

I have pleasure in expressing my deepest gratitude to Dr. Jascha-Alexander Koch for his friendly, patient and expert help in transcribing Diaries 2 and 3, without which this book could not have been compiled.

Thanks to Bloomsbury Publishing for their kind permission to reproduce extracts from 'The Italian Campaign' of Michael Hickey's *The First World War (4): The Mediterranean Front 1915-1923*, Essential Histories 23. Osprey Publishing, 2003.

Thanks to The Orion Publishing Group, London, for their kind permission to reproduce extracts from *Wittgenstein's Vienna* Copyright © 1973 by Allan Janik and Stephen Toulmin.

Thanks are due also to:
- my cousins Peter Brier and Esti Gavry, for information about their side of the family and our grandparents;
- Val Ionta, who translated from Italian some of the letters and postcards written by and to Severin;
- Michael Brett for permission to use a photo from his collection of banknotes from the place and time relating to this book;
- Barry Swain for giving me and allowing me to use General Haig's War Bulletin from 1917;
- libreria_il_tempo_che_fu for providing me with and giving me permission to use two photos of Val Frenzela;
- my old friend Pat Geelan, former Secretary of the UK's Permanent Committee on Geographical Names, for attempting to identify some of the places named in the diaries.

I owe particular gratitude to:
- Keith Foskett ('Fozzie'), who provided indispensable help in getting this book published;
- Dușan Arsenić, who designed the book jacket;
- Jason Anderson of Polgarus, who designed the layout.

I am deeply grateful also to my close and extended family and friends who have offered encouragement and expressed their keen interest in seeing this book.

Colours have been used to distinguish different elements of the book.

Black: Preliminary pages, Acknowledgements, Genesis of this book, Biography of Severin Breier and the diary entries themselves (dates in red)

Blue: Background information from external sources and Editor's notes

Green: Translations of letters, postcards, documents and some lengthier captions

Severin Breier: A Biography

Severin Breier (in his youth nicknamed Nino) was born on 2 May 1898 in Lemberg, now Lviv, Ukraine. The family moved to Vienna when he was two. At that time, Ukraine, Austria and many areas of what is now northern Italy were part of the Austro-Hungarian Empire. Severin's sister, Charlotte (Lotte), was born in 1902 and his two brothers, Franz and Walter, in 1904 and 1908, respectively. Their parents, Simon (also known as Salomon) and Ernestine, had their own business designing and manufacturing dolls' clothing. Ernestine's designs were highly regarded, and they provided the principal asset of the business.

The Austro-Hungarian Empire in 1914
Source: https://www.quora.com/What-territories-belonged-to-the-Kingdom-of-Hungary-in-Austria-Hungary

The family, having moved to Vienna, retained their links with and allegiance to Lemberg. Indeed, it seems that, as late as 1916, Simon Breier was seeking validation of his citizenship of Lemberg [see letter on Adolf Steinberg headed paper].

ADOLF STEINBERG
ENGLISCHE
SCHUHNIEDERLAGE.

Lemberg, 8. August 1916,
Haliczergasse 19.
abends.

Teure Eltern!

Habe vorgestern früh Mamas l. Karte erhalten u. komme erst jetzt dazu, Euch zu antworten. Den Empfang des vorigen Picketes u. wie gut alles war, habe ich im verlorengegangenen Briefe beschrieben u. da Ihr meinen Dank hiefür nicht erhalten habt, so danke ich jetzt nochmals. Mir geht es so wie immer oder noch mehr wie immer recht gut. Anfang nächster Woche dürfte ein guter Kamerad von mir nach Wien kommen. Fraget ihn nur aus! Er war immer mit mir zusammen, seit ich beim Regiment bin. Sein Name ist Griffel. Heute war Tischebow u. da wurden alle Juden des Regim. gemeinsam vor- u. nachmittags zum Gottesdienste geführt; die übrigbleibende Zeit hatten wir dienstfrei. Bei dieser Gelegenheit bemerkte ich, dass unter den gesamten Einjährigen mehr Juden als Christen sind. Was Deine Heimatsangelegenheiten betrifft,

8 August 1916, evening

Dearest Parents!

I received Mama's lovely card in the morning the day before yesterday, and only now have the chance to reply to you. In my last letters, which went missing, I wrote that I had received the last packet and how good everything was, and as you did not receive my thanks for it, I thank you again now. Everything is fine with me as usual, or even better than usual. At the beginning of next week a good friend of mine should be arriving in Vienna. Ask him whatever you want! We have been together the whole time, ever since I joined the Regiment. His name is Griffel. Today was Tisha B'Av and all Jews in the Regiment were taken both in the morning and in the afternoon to religious service; the rest of the time I was free. On this occasion I noticed that there are more Jews than Christians among the One-Year Volunteers.

As regards the matter of your homeland, dear Papa, the request has been lodged. The grant notice regarding your request for jurisdiction was dealt with under No. 67670/16 on 27.5. This is probably still with reference to citizenship in Lemberg. Perhaps you can (so a Magistrate has told me) discover the number under which your second request (for citizenship in Vienna) has been dealt with. Enclosed is a newspaper, which may perhaps interest you or the children. Robert was still in Lemberg until yesterday but he probably left this afternoon.

I have received a letter from Aunt Salka, in which she writes that Otto is at present in Namur, but will probably be transferred soon to Valenciennes. She also asks whether I would prefer a parcel or pocket money. I hope dear Uncle Adolf will be kind enough to reply to this letter (enclosed) from Auntie. The Schneier family have received your letter, with thanks, and have asked me to send you warm greetings, before they are able to write to you themselves. I have read the letter too and find it so superbly well thought out that I am sure it will be rated a success.

I expect your letter tomorrow!

Many countless kisses and greetings from your devoted son, Severin.

Please pass on my greetings to everyone!

VIENNA IN THE 1900s

Extracts and information from Allan Janis and Stephen Toulmin: *Wittgenstein's Vienna*. London: Weidenfeld & Nicholson, 1973.

Wittgenstein's Vienna was "a paradox of stagnation and ferment that took place within the context of a crumbling, scandal-ridden autocracy, run as a tyranny leavened by frivolity, and a society conscious of the gathering storm of its own incompetence."

By the standards of the late 19th century, Austria-Hungary (also known as the Dual Monarchy or the House of Habsburg) was one of the acknowledged superpowers, having a vast territory, a well-established power structure and a long record of apparent constitutional stability.

Between 1890 and 1919, major developments were taking place, all concentrated in Vienna: the emergence of psychoanalysis, the beginnings of the Bauhaus school of architecture, non-representational painting by the artists of the Secession, who separated themselves from the established activities of orthodox academic art, and the stirrings of 'legal positivism' in the jurisprudence of Hans Kelsen (author of *The Pure Theory of Law*).

Vienna prided itself on its image as the City of Dreams, but was described by the satirist, polemicist and critic Karl Kraus as the 'Proving-ground for World Destruction'. Though renowned for its music, its dancing and its coffee houses, Vienna had a dark side, including a grave housing shortage that persisted even after WWII. Musicians and composers and other innovators were, if 'Semitic', denounced as degenerates and proclaimed cultural heroes only after their deaths. Similarly, at the turn of the century, Vienna was the medical centre of the world, but the pioneering work of Freud in psychoanalysis and Semmelweiss on infection went unrecognised because their contemporaries were too poorly informed and lacked the vision to appreciate the significance of their work.

Both Nazism and German anti-Semitism had their origins in the Old Vienna, as did certain elements of modern Catholic thought and what may be termed 'Austria-Marxism'.

An effort to replace Latin with German so as to streamline imperial administration "begat Hungarian and Czech nationalism", which in turn begat political nationalism. "Slav nationalism in politics and economics in turn begat German economic and political nationalism; and this in is turn begat anti-Semitism, with Zionism as a natural reaction" (pp. 39–40).

The external splendours of Vienna at the turn of the century were largely the work of Emperor Franz Joseph, who rebuilt the city between 1858 and 1888: the Ringstrasse, a new Imperial Palace and the two museums opposite it, a new Reichstag building, the opera house and an imperial theatre.

Nevertheless, Vienna was above all a city of the bourgeoisie, with their penchant for stability, making a 'good marriage', their imitation of the past among the nouveau riche. "Viennese of the generation that reached maturity at the beginning of the century were raised ... in an atmosphere so saturated with, and devoted to, 'aesthetic values' that they were scarcely able to comprehend that any other values existed at all" (p. 44). Earlier, business, money-making and law and order were the preoccupations of the bourgeoisie. Now, art became a way of life, as did writing for e.g. *Die Neue Freie Presse*, which offered a relief from the repression of the previous and present generations.

Women had suffered particularly from the patriarchy of society, being forced to wear cumbersome clothing to conceal and subdue their sexuality. Women were not expected to be educated beyond what was essential to 'good breeding'. Men too were constrained by custom to remain unmarried until they reached social maturity at the age of 25 or 26, and therefore found sexual outlet with prostitutes.

Liberalism tended to be confined to middle-class Germans and German Jews of the urban centres. Instead, mass movements arose and alongside them Viennese aestheticism. By the time of WWI, Vienna's population of two million included 200,000 Czechs. The most thriving political groups in Vienna were working-class movements led by defectors from liberalism.

The rapid growth of Vienna's population, from less than half a million in 1857 to over two million in 1910, worsened an already severe housing problem. By 1910, the average dwelling housed 4.4 persons, with an average of 1.24 per room (including kitchen, bathroom and front hallway). Only 1.2% of the population lived in single-family homes and only 22% of dwellings had indoor toilets.

In the depression between the Bourse crash of 1873 and the late 1890s, anti-Semitism rose as the stock market fell. Jewish 'capitalists' were accused of corruption and profiteering.

Strangely, both the Nazis' Final Solution and the idea of a Zionist state originated in Vienna. Although very few Jews could enter the elite, many compensated by entering the cultural aristocracy, escaping from the life of trade to which they were otherwise destined. There were Jews in every class except the high aristocracy, the military and the civil service. By 1910 they constituted 5% of the population and made up the largest portion of the medical, legal and journalistic professions.

Arthur Schnitzler, a physician turned playwright, considered anti-Semitism to be one manifestation of the human condition, a symptom of a universal spiritual malaise. People cannot communicate "because they encapsulate themselves hopelessly within social roles which satisfy their immediate desires, and thereby rob themselves of all hope of more lasting fulfilment" (p. 63). "If the Habsburg Empire's national, racial, social, diplomatic and sexual problems were as grave as we have suggested, the Empire's suicide rate should have been correspondingly high" (p. 64). And it was.

In 1907, universal manhood suffrage was introduced in the western half of the monarchy. The Czechs could no longer communicate with the Germans, because the Germans failed to recognise the Czech language. ... language was the basis of social as well as political identity in the bitter struggles for civil rights which marked the final years of Habsburg rule before the cataclysm of 1914 (p. 65).

The new aesthetes "sought in their poetry a more "authentic" language, one that would allow them to escape from the straitjacket of bourgeois society" (p. 66).

"Anti-Semitic writers later [after the death by suicide of Otto Weininger, author of *Sex and Character*] asserted that Weininger was the wisest of Jews: when he realised the impossibility both of assimilation and of continuing to live as a Jew in non-Jewish society, he chose the only reasonable solution to his dilemma; believing as he did that the Jewish character was by nature the lowest, most depraved type of character... and that all character was eternal and immutable, he had no alternative" (p. 71).

The family was consciously but not observantly Jewish. In his youth, Severin did attend synagogue on significant days in the Jewish calendar, such as Yom Kippur, but no other rituals appear to have been followed.

From 1904 to probably 1908, Severin was a pupil at the Allgemeine Volkschule in Wien für Knaben, XV, Viktoriagasse 2 [Elementary School for Boys in Vienna], which was across the road from where the family lived at Viktoriagasse 1. His school reports, of which the elementary school reports were signed by his father as Salomon Breier, were on the whole very favourable, notably with respect to his behaviour, which was always admirable.

Severin in 1912, aged 14

A school report from 1904

In school he learned a form of shorthand called Gabelsberger, created c. 1817 by Franz Xavier Gabelsberger and widely used between 1834, when it was first fully described, and 1924, when it ceased to be taught. Severin, however, continued to use this shorthand all his life.

In 1915 he was already undergoing military training. Severin was essentially a pacifist – he said that he never knowingly hurt or killed anyone during his wartime service, and he always shot to miss! (In light of his poor target shooting, it is possible that his shots that were aimed to miss actually hit a target.)

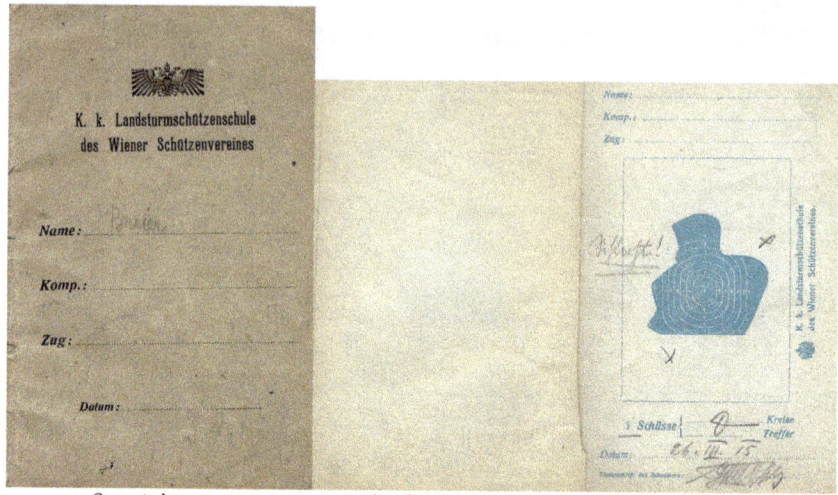

Severin's target practice record. The instructor's comment reads 'Bad'.

Ration cards
70g bread or 50g flour, totalling 490g bread or 350g flour, week 38, 26.12.1915 to 1.1.1916. These must have been issued to citizens, as they predate Severin's enlistment into the army later in 1916.

In 1916, when he turned 18, driven probably by a sense of duty and patriotism, he requested to enlist in the Replacement Training Battalion of Infantry Regiment No. 64 of the K.u.K. army as a One-Year Volunteer. The request was refused. Nevertheless, Severin did join up as a One-Year Volunteer, in the K.u.K. Infantry Regiment No. 41.

Request to enlist

Request to enlist in the K.u.K. Infantry Regiment No. 64 as a One-Year Volunteer
To the K.u.K. Reserve Division of Inf. Reg. No. 64

Vienna, 19 April 1916   Vienna XII

The undersigned takes the liberty of requesting to enlist in the K.u.K. Inf. Reg. No. 64 as a One-Year Volunteer. Born in and a citizen of Lemberg, he was found suitable at the army medical for the year 1898. He is at present in the eighth class at the Stadtgymnasium in the VII district of Vienna.

Severin Breier,
Vienna XV, Viktoriagasse 1

His training appears to have taken place at a number of sites within striking distance of Vienna. One such was Marienfeld, near Jägerndorf (now Krnov, Czech Republic), in autumn 1916.

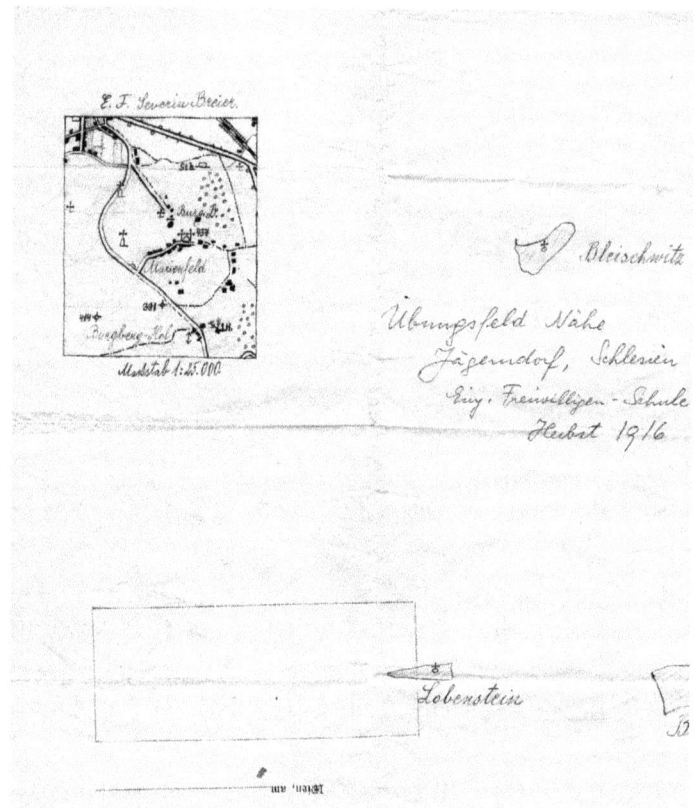

Practice field, near Jägerndorf, Silesia (now Krnov, Czech Republic),
One-year Volunteers, autumn 1916

Bleischwitz now Bliszczyce, southwestern Poland, just across the border from Krnov
Branitz now Branice, in southwestern Poland, near the Czech border, still close to Krnov
Lobenstein or Selenburk now Cvilin, and Marienfeld now Marienské Pole, just south of Krnov

Authorisation 19/9/1916:
To go into town during his free time and to sleep outside the barracks.
However, not to stay out over the [?] retreat.

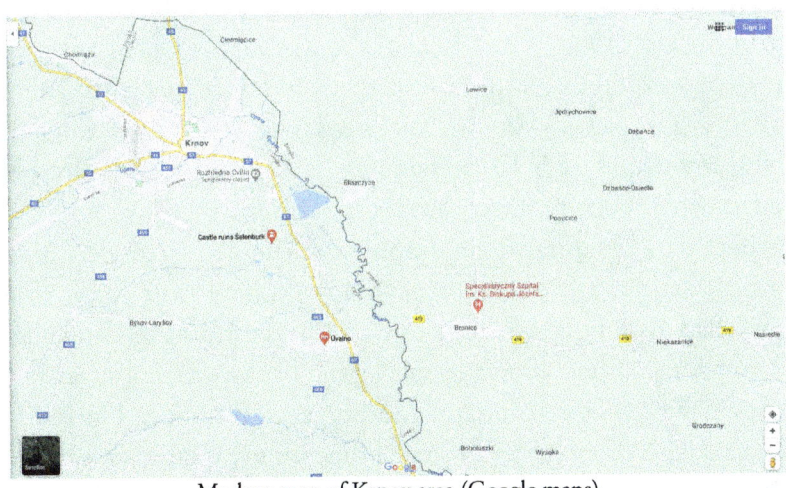

Modern map of Krnov area (Google maps)

In April 1917, Severin was in what is now Romania, aged only 19 already training other soldiers in the arts of battle, including the use of bayonets and hand grenades.

[Translation of letter of which some pages are reproduced below.]

27/IV/1917

Dearest father!

As you can see, I'm keeping my promise to write a long letter as soon as possible, so it may be that this letter arrives at the same time as the two cards. Today I have more time than usual anyway, as there are no duties in the afternoon. The whole of the week there were concerts and evenings of entertainment put on in the town, to which the One-Year Volunteers got passes. So on Wednesday I went into town after finishing my duties at 5.30, arriving at 7. After I had bought what I needed most, I went (with comrades, of course, there were five of us altogether) to a restaurant for dinner and then to a concert and tea evening. It started at 8pm, there was no specified time for it to end, but, as I had to report for duty early the next morning, I decided at 12.30 to go back; two comrades had gone back earlier and, as for the other two, who were going to another acquaintance, I missed the rendezvous with them, so I had to go home on my own; luckily I caught a lift in a car that was heading for our village and was home in an hour. Of course I didn't get a decent amount of sleep until the night afterwards. So today, on the occasion of the name day of our Empress, the 43rd Music Ensemble came to our village and there was entertainment, combined with military music. You could see soldiers there from all possible regiments, Germans, Hungarians, Romanians, you name it. It was rather fun.

You have asked about what I do every day. We are now actually being properly drilled, i.e. the troops; there is daily practice in the use of small weapons, bayonet combat and throwing hand grenades. The troops have to undergo scrupulous instruction, so that they don't become like machines that simply fulfil the purpose for which they were made, rather that each man thinks and if necessary acts independently. Accomplishing this is the job of the One-Year Volunteers. In this I am hampered by my lack of knowledge of the Romanian language; for that reason, there is always an interpreter on hand who translates what I say.

We are fully outfitted and armed by 6.30am. It is not far to the exercise ground and we get there before 7am. It is in the forest; we don't practise the same things every day but ring the changes. We are back again at 11am. In the afternoon we are off duty at 1.30 and at 5pm we report for service. Orders are then given.

The food is now very good. In the morning black coffee, but really rich, sweet, black coffee, not that brown watery stuff that you get for example at railway station kiosks. For the midday meal we get soup, namely vegetable or cabbage soup, beef every day, which is well cooked and served with such dishes as mămăligă [a porridge made out of yellow maize flour, traditional dish of Romania, Moldova and West Ukraine], cabbage with turnips, turnips cooked in roux or similar. In the evening coffee with something extra; yesterday the extra was sardines, the day before it was sausage, today it is marmalade. But the main thing is that we also get what is essential to accompany the sausage or the marmalade, etc., namely bread. We get half a loaf every day, only exceptionally sometimes a quarter loaf, the other quarter being replaced by rusks. In addition, we have drinks, namely good-quality wine, rum, rum with syrup, the syrup according to whatever is allocated to us by the provisions centre. So I have no complaints either about the food.

A marching battalion from another regiment is also quartered in our village. Our company has some 5–6 small houses assigned to it, where four platoons and the company command are accommodated. Three One-Year

Volunteers, of whom I am one, live together with a few of the 1ˢᵗ Company in a large attic room of a small house. The housekeeper often brings us eggs, potatoes and milk. My laundry gets done in the house.

My only wish would be to have a proper bath; but that's not available even in town.

I am receiving copious news from many friends and relatives, e.g. Uncle Heinrich, Uncle Dolfi [Adolf], and further from Pfeffer, from my Hickinger [?] class. Has Uncle Heinrich written to tell you if he was in Kattowitz [Katowice]? I am sure Aunt Salka will not feel bound to pick up a pen even now. I write to the aunts in Lemberg, of course.

I often receive 5–6 cards on the same day, which makes me very happy. Needless to say, the cards from you and Mama and the children bring me the greatest pleasure. So, enough!

With affectionate greetings and kisses

Your devoted son, Severin

Pages 1 and 8 of Severin's letter to his father from a training camp
27 April 1917

Pages 2 and 7 of Severin's letter to his father from a training camp
27 April 1917

SUGGEST THE REAL EXPLANATION

of this lull. The German newspapers are making out that our spring offensive has definitely failed, and that it is therefore finished. Their talent for misinterpretation and miscalculation remains unquenchable.

British prisoners who have made their way back to our lines say the enemy is manifestly very short of various necessities of war. Their gas masks were all taken from them, the explanation for which is that owing to the rubber famine the German respirators are much inferior to our own. This gives point to the news that several times during the past week we have released gas waves against the people who first introduced this method of waging war. All the motor transport these men saw had iron tyres.

I am of opinion that the mobile reserves of the enemy have probably been depleted to an even greater degree than we have reason to suspect.—Reuter.

AUSTRIANS DEMORALISED

SIGNIFICANT ADMISSIONS BY CAPTURED TROOPS.

Austrian prisoners taken on the Julian front declare that the Italian offensive has been irresistible and far more powerful than the Austrian commanders expected. All possible means were employed by the Austrian commands to assure the soldiers that no Italian efforts would be able to shake the Austrian defences. Most of the prisoners taken state that they had only been on the Italian front for a very short time, having been brought from the Russian and Roumanian fronts. They assert that if the Russians were to attack now in the Carpathians they would speedily have Hungary at their mercy. General conditions in Austria, they say, are terrible, and Austria cannot possibly resist much longer. The food distributed to the Austrian troops is incredibly bad, and they get practically no meat. The harvest prospects in Austria and Hungary are even worse than last year, there being but few peasants to work the land. The conquest of Roumania has been a great disappointment to Austria, because the Germans and Bulgarians have taken all that there was to take. It is also stated by prisoners that there are now no German troops on the Italian front, they having been taken to France, but there are still a number of Bulgarian and Turkish troops and a few German detachments behind the Austrian lines. General Arz is in command of the Austrian forces on the Italian front, and he is assisted by General Conrad. The latter, however, does not hold any definite position.—Central News.

THE SINGLE FRONT.

LINE RANGING FROM NORTH SEA TO PERSIA.

The war is so vast that there is a tendency to regard each of the campaigns as separable from the rest. Really the battle front is continuous. The following, says a Student of the War, in the "Manchester Guardian," may serve as a conspectus of the war, disposed in the order of a single battle, with the orthodox three divisions into left, centre, and right:—

Left Wing.—Our communications at sea: The German object is to interrupt our communications with the United States so as to hamper the transport of supplies to the western offensive and to prevent the Americans from sending troops to France.

Centre.—The British and French offensive in the West. In the military, though not in the geographical, sense, the Russo-German front in Courland belongs to this division, because any pressure that the Russians might exercise here would have an immediate effect in drawing off Germans from France.

Right.—This section of the battle is geographically the most extensive of all, extending as it does from the Isonzo to Persia, and from the Pripet Marshes and the Caucasus to Gaza. It subdivides quite naturally into three sections—a western, which includes the Italian offensive, the Austro-Russian front in Galicia, and the Allied front in Macedonia; a middle section, to which the British offensive in Palestine and the Russian occupation of the Caucasus belong; and an eastern sec

day, and usually goes about in military uniform. At 8 o'clock there is dinner, consisting in the Lent week referred to of four courses, including fish. Usually, half a bottle of red wine is placed on the table, but nobody touches it, and the bottle travels back to the cellar unopened. The dinner is charged at 4 roubles 50 kopecks per person.

The Grand Duke Alexis, being ill, has his meals in bed, and usually chooses his own dishes. Twice a day the entire family gathers in the church, but here, too, the

TSAR IS SEPARATED FROM HIS WIFE.

The Tsaritsa comes down from the staircase, and is taken to the church in an invalid chair. She takes her place behind a screen and kneels down in devout prayer.

At 11 o'clock at night tea is served, and at 1 o'clock everybody goes to bed. The ex-Tsar gives the impression of a man totally indifferent to his fate; at least, he shows no signs of uneasiness or agitation. The Tsaritsa is exceedingly reserved. With a cold and impassive face and tightly closed lips she resembles a marble statue. She has betrayed her feelings only once, when she was parted from her favourite maid-in-waiting, Madame Vyroubov. Then she broke into sobs, and cried for several minutes. The whole day the Tsaritsa and her daughters are busily sewing underclothing for wounded soldiers. The correspondence of the Tsar and Tsaritsa is strictly controlled, and even their interviews with members of the former entourage, who are interned in the same palace, take place in the presence of wardens. Alexis is always in the company of his favourite man-servant and a French tutor. The Tsaritsa is in a sort of religious trance. She has a mass of religious literature, such as the devotional booklets of John of Kronstadt. Her correspondence is also generally of a religious character, being carried on for the most part on postcards with religious pictures. She usually signs herself by her initial "A," to which is added a cross.

WASTE NOT, WANT NOT.

Bread is the staff of life, but you can whittle the staff if you have a patriotic stomach. Eat less bread—save a pound a week. This is a tip from the stable, and should be followed.

THE HUN'S EFFRONTERY.

MEDITERRANEAN TO BE CLOSED TO HOSPITAL SHIPS.

Amsterdam, May 26.—A German memorandum relative to the alleged use of hospital ships by the Allies for the conveyance of troops and war materiel announces that the German Government has decided to prevent enemy hospital ship traffic

"GOING THE SAME WAY HOME."

far regiment of American infantry war of 1898.

THE OFFICERS WERE HIGHLY INTELLI

and their handiness and resourceful the result of their Indian experien made a delightful combination with

exceptional mental equipment. In journey by train through almost the e length of the United States the men allowed freely to roam about the rail stations when the train stopped, as it quently did, yet there was not a single of drunkenness, though the regiment just said "Good-bye" to its friends was under the excitement of the approa ing campaign. The train passed thr "dry" States and "wet" States, but wet States were just as dry as the dr far as that regiment was concerned. present writer remarked on the exem behaviour of the men under so little trol, and one of the officers said to h "Why I expect you would find that could take any man out of this regi and safely make him a cashier in a ba

THE CHILDREN'S WAR.

This is the Children's War because
The victory's to the young and cle
Up to the Dragon's ravening jaws
Match dear Eighteen and Sevent

O men with many scars and stains,
Stand back, abase your souls and p
For now to Nineteen are the gains
And golden Twenty wins the day.

Brown heads with curls all rippled
Young bodies slender as a flame;
They leap to darkness like a lover—
To Twenty-one is tall'n the game.

It is the Boy's War. Praise be given
To Perevale and Galahad,
Who have won earth and taken Heav
By violence! Weep not, but be gl
Katharine Tynan, in the "Spectato

THE HUN BY THE HOME FIRE

Herr Kaiser, the German public p cutor for youthful criminals, said Munich meeting that criminality au the young had increased enormously ing the war, not only in Munich, bu all the large towns. There had nearly a 100 per cent. increase in tences.

He emphasised the increase in robb malicious woundings, and inu offences. Much of the degeneration ascribed to the high wages earned youths under 18.

Very often they bully their mother sisters while their father is in the a and refuse to contribute towards ho hold expenses, wasting their wage riotous living.

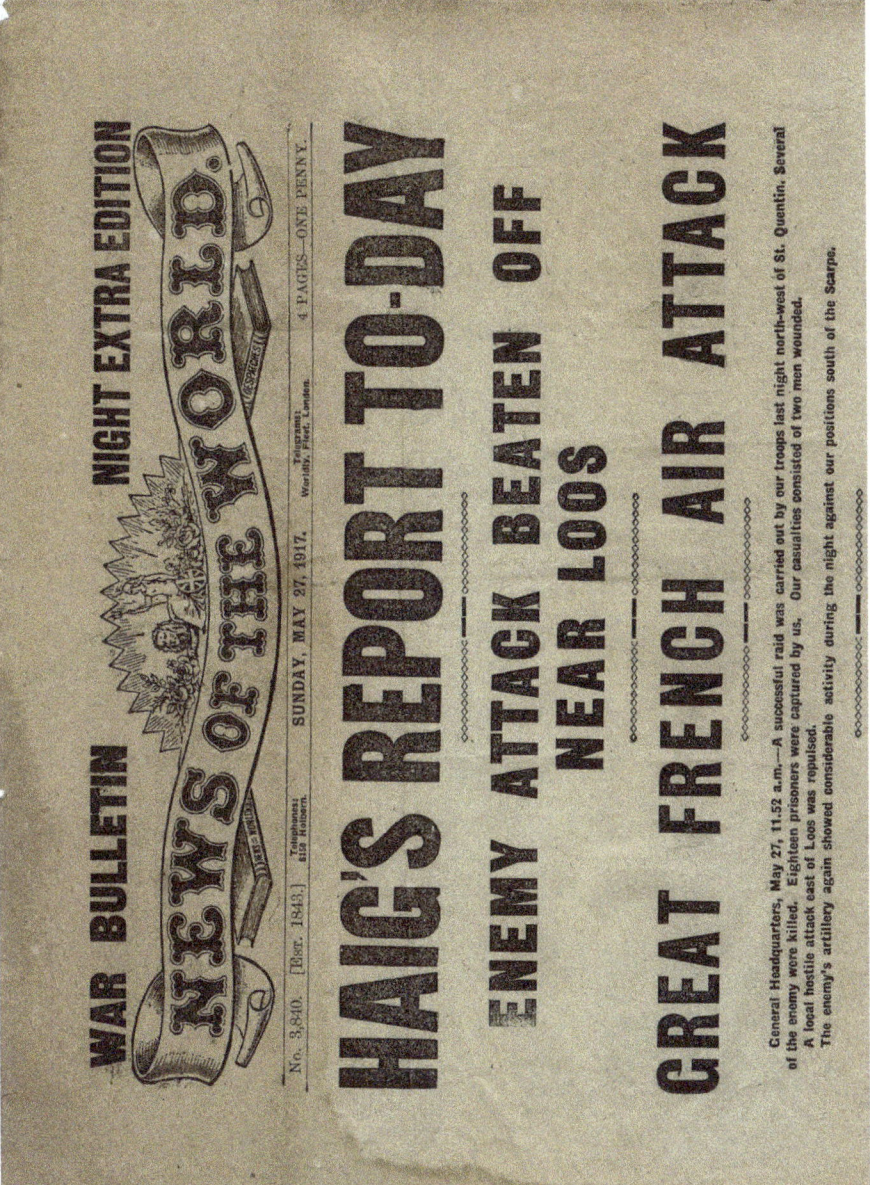

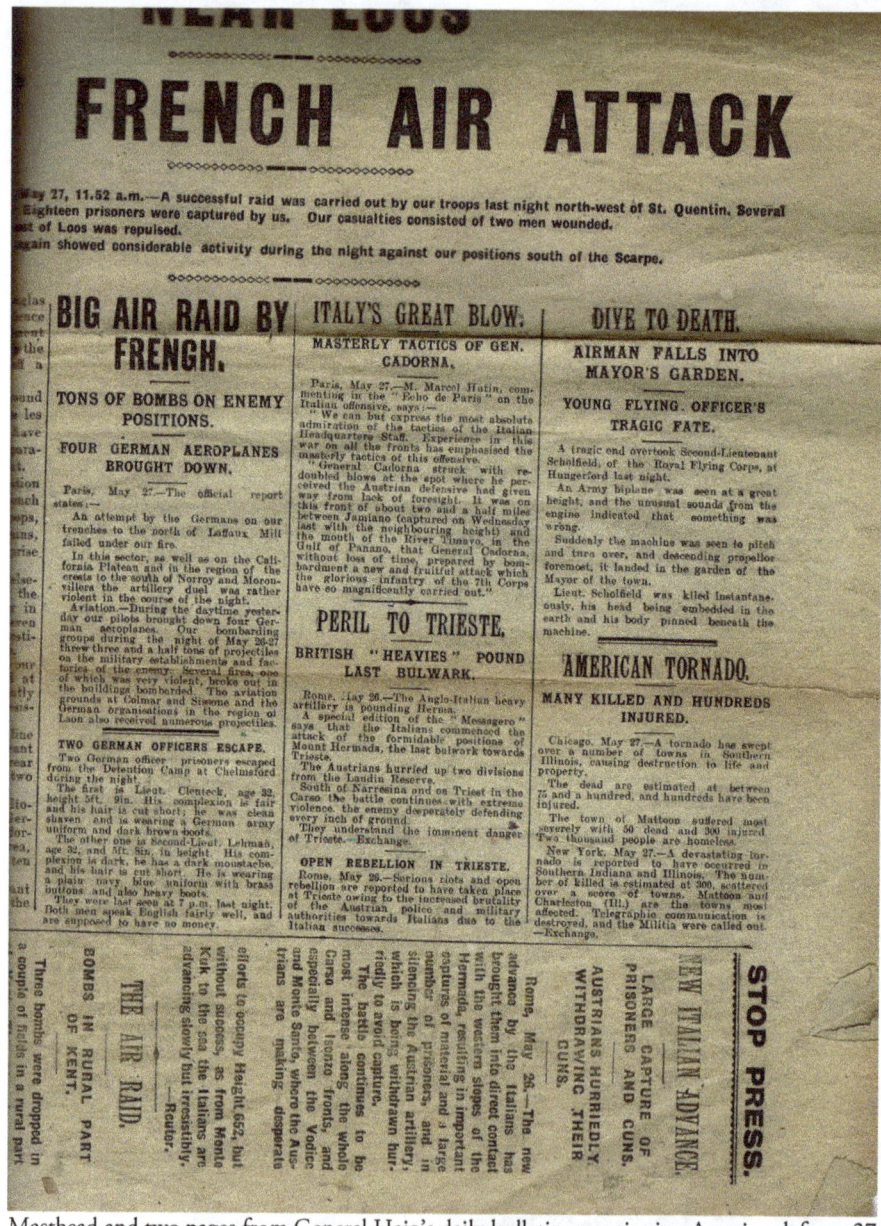

Masthead and two pages from General Haig's daily bulletin, mentioning Austrian defeats, 27 May 1917 (three images). Courtesy Barry Swain private collection

It is not known when Severin was sent to the front. However, DIARY 1 covers the period from 1 August to 14 October 1917, including his engagement in the 11th Battle of Isonzo, as a member of the 117th Infantry Regiment. The Isonzo (now called Soča) river rises in the Trenta Valley in the Julian Alps in northwestern Slovenia, at an elevation of 876 metres, and flows south to enter the Adriatic Sea at Trieste. There were 12 Battles of Isonzo, fiercely fought between the Austro-Hungarians and the Italians.

Extracts from Michael Hickey: *The First World War (4): The Mediterranean Front 1915-1923*, Essential Histories 23. Oxford: Osprey Publishing, 2003, pp. 60-65: The Italian Campaign.
Reproduced with kind permission from Bloomsbury Publishing.

The Austro-Italian frontier had been created artificially by a Treaty in 1866 engineered by Bismarck, providing Austria with a barrier of mountains from which her army could sweep down at will onto the north Italian Plain. Any Italian offensive would have to be conducted uphill. Italy's difficulties were increased by the shape of the frontier, a giant 'S' on its side, with a huge salient projecting into Italy in the Trentino district, and the Udine salient extending into Austrian territory. Of these the Trentino was potentially the more dangerous, but its poor road and rail communications also presented problems to Austria's military planners. From the Swiss border to the Adriatic the battle line extended for nearly 400 miles, divided into three segments: Trentino, Alpine, and Isonzo. Except for about 30 moderately hilly miles on the Isonzo, the entire line lay in mountain terrain. Anticipating war with Austria, whose intentions towards her former Venetian provinces were all too clear, Italy had fortified all three fronts, covering the northern Plain with a network of strategic roads and railways to permit rapid movement of troops to any threatened sector.

On their side of the frontier the Austrian General Staff had constructed permanent defensive positions and had improved the transportation infrastructure in the rear areas. The existence of fixed defences on both sides dictated that from the outset the campaign would be mainly static. The Italian Chief of Staff General Cadorna planned to attack on the Isonzo front, where the objectives of Trieste and the route to Vienna lay within reach, along with the tempting opportunity to link with the armies of Serbia and Russia. The Italians' Achilles heel was the Trentino front, where a successful Austrian breakthrough would isolate Cadorna's armies on the Isonzo. The lay-out of the Italian railway system in the region acknowledged this; a double-track route ran parallel to the frontier, with spurs branching off up the valleys. The Austrian rail system provided a main line following their side of the frontier but was deficient in branch lines, and this was eventually to lose them the momentum of their offensive in Trentino.

On the outbreak of hostilities the Italians deployed 35 divisions, facing some 20 Austrian divisions in strong, near-impregnable positions along the front. Soldiers of both sides faced arduous conditions in the mountains. Cadorna planned a sustained offensive on the Isonzo and aggressive defence on the Trentino, whilst securing advantageous positions for his *Alpini* fighting in the high Carnic Alps.

… … …

In their first four Isonzo attacks alone the Italians lost 161,000 men and the Austrians nearly 147,000 killed, wounded, captured and missing.

… … …

As winter descended the tempo of operations slowed, and cholera, supposedly contracted from the Austrians, spread through the Italian army. The Italians were still short of artillery, especially the heavy guns needed to break up the Austrian defences. At an Allied summit conference at Chantilly it was agreed that Britain and France would provide additional guns and equipment to buttress the Italian war effort. The Austrian Chief of Staff, Conrad, was expected by his German Allies to concentrate his main efforts against the Russians, freeing German formations for use on the Western Front. But he had ideas of his own. One was to mount a decisive attack in the Trentino, advancing rapidly across the Italian Plain to seize the great cities of the north. He selected the area around the Asiago plateau for the attack.

… … …

the Chief of the German General Staff, General Erich von Falkenhayn, believed that the 18 divisions assembled by Conrad would prove inadequate, even though the Austrians enjoyed a marked superiority in artillery – 2,000 guns including nearly 500 pieces of heavy artillery against the Italians' 588 field and 36 heavy guns. The Trentino attack began at dawn on 15 May 1916, using the novelty of a short but concentrated artillery bombardment that virtually destroyed the Italian trench systems. The Austrian heavy artillery was devastating in the confined valleys, causing avalanches and rock falls; but the rugged terrain saved the Italians from overwhelming defeat, as it slowed the Austrian advance to a crawl.

… … …

In January 1917, the Russian Revolution, beginning in March, enabled the Austrians to transfer formations from the east to augment their forces on the Isonzo and Trentino fronts. Undeterred, Cadorna ordered two further attacks, the 10th and 11th, on the Isonzo. At the end of August the Italians seemed on the point of final victory; Austrian morale was crumbling as non-Germanic regiments lost their stomach for the war. The Allies had responded to Cadorna's pleas for heavy artillery and British 6-inch batteries were serving under his command.

… … …

12th Isonzo, or Caporetto as it became known, had been a catastrophe. The Italians lost 10,000 killed, 30,000 wounded, a staggering 265,000 taken prisoner, and untold thousands of deserters. Losses of equipment were equally calamitous: over 3,000 guns, 3,000 machine guns, almost 2,000 mortars, and vast quantities of stores and equipment.

… … …

Throughout the spring and summer of 1918, as matters hung in the balance in France, the Italian front was quiet; General Armando Diaz [who had replaced Cadorno], determined to give his army time to recover from Caporetto, declined to attack until ordered to do so by Premier Orlando in October. By now the Italians had been augmented by significant French and British forces. Orlando believed an attack now was essential in order to gain bargaining power at the conference table – all the signs indicated that the Austro-Hungarian empire was about to collapse. The offensive launched by Diaz on 24 October proved Orlando correct. As the Allied army attacked at Vittorio Veneto the Austrians broke and ran. A rout ensued, with mutiny and mass desertions by Serbian, Croatian, Czech and Polish troops. Mutiny also broke out in the Austrian navy and on 3 November Austria signed armistice terms. The war in Italy was over.

Following a period of (presumably) more military engagement and training, for example in Császárkőbánya, now known as Kaisersteinbruch, Severin found himself in a different part of northern Italy, to the east of Lake Garda.

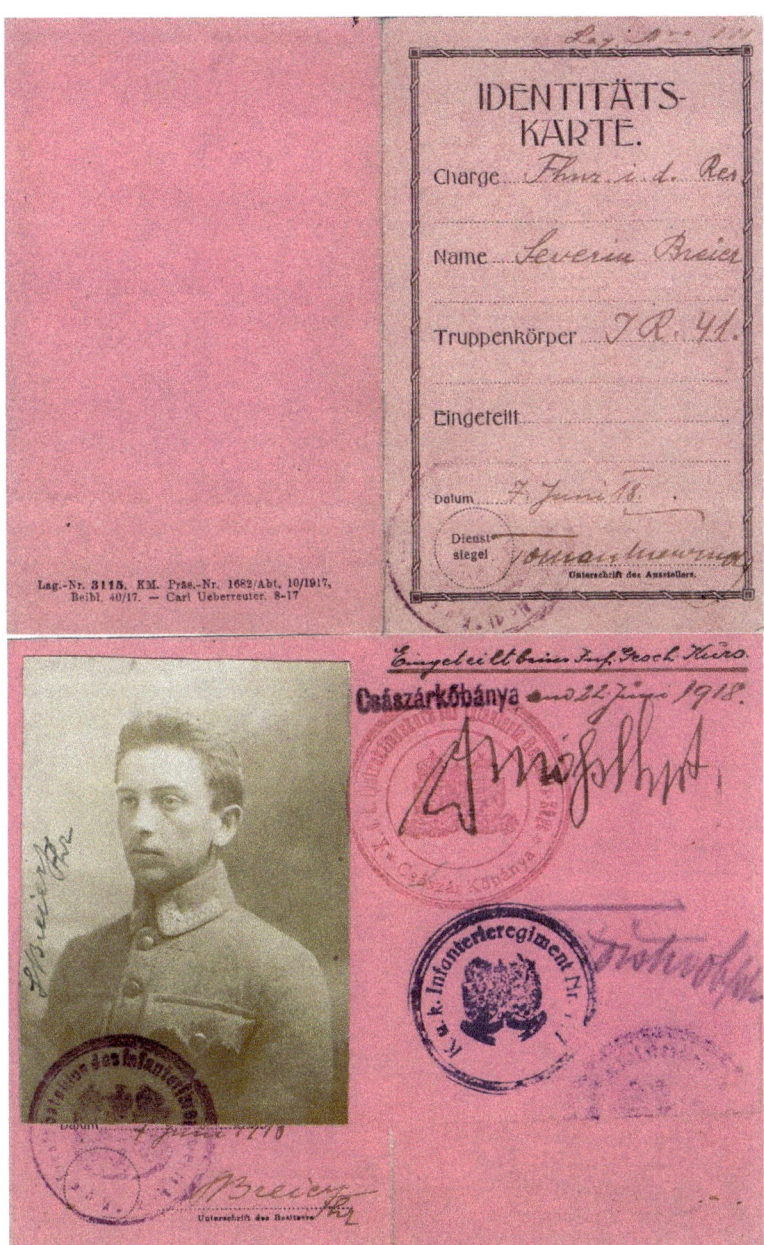

ID for assignment to a course on the History of the Infantry, June 1918. Császárkőbánya, known in German as Kaisersteinbruch, is about 55km SE of Vienna. There was a military camp there. In 1939 it became the site of one of the first POW internment camps in the entire German Reich, Stalag XVIIA.

Letter from Severin's father from Dabrowe (now Dąbrowa Górnicza, southern Poland), 26/2/1918

By this time, Severin was in Lemberg (now Lviv), probably still undergoing training or in preparation for going to the front.

The letter is written in the old-fashioned German handwriting, and starts 'Mein geliebter Severin!' [my beloved Severin].

He refers to having received three cards on the 22nd. He is glad that Severin is in Lemberg. He describes his own residence [he is probably there on business] and mentions that he eats in the canteen, which is cheap. He thanks God that he is well and fit. He refers to Uncle Heinrich, whose regiment is in Krakau [Krakow] and says that perhaps he will be able to come and visit.

He concludes by saying that he is happy that Severin is well and sends many warm kisses from his 'loving Papa'. The afterscript refers to giving greetings to Grandmother.

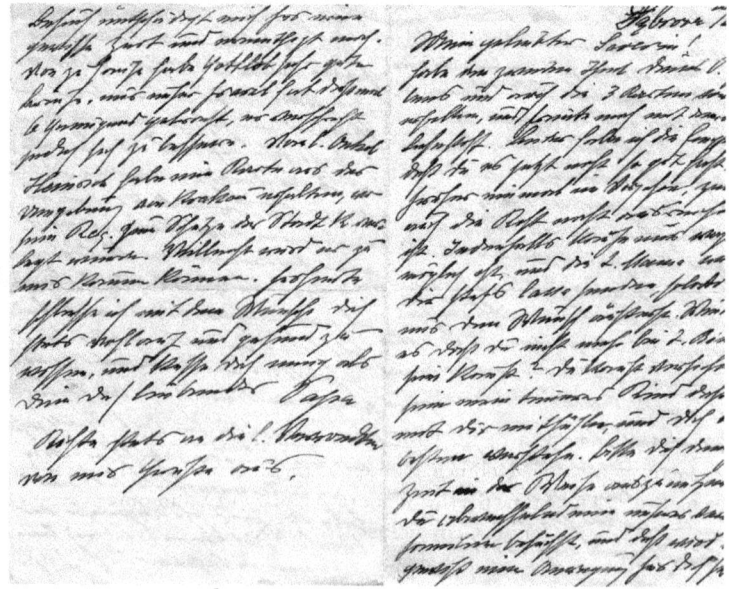

Letter from Severin's father, 26 February 1918

Letter from family on promotion

Vienna 11/III/1918

A letter [previous page] written on the occasion of Severin's promotion to Ensign (approximate equivalent Second Lieutenant). Extracts below are from various contributors to the letter, including:
- a friend, 'B', who wrote to 'My dearest golden' boy;
- Severin's brother Walter, then aged about 10, to his 'beloved brother' and signed with 'heartiest greetings from your loving brother';
- Berta [an aunt?];
- Severin's other brother Franz, then aged about 14, addressed to 'Dear Herr officer' and signed with '10,000,000 greetings and kisses';
- Severin's sister Lotte, then aged about 16, writing that 'The best comes last' and 'My pride in you is enormous', and 'Count the hairs in your moustache, your eyelashes and your eyebrows and for every one I send you a kiss' from 'your Lotte'.

Telegram from Severin's father to greet Severin on his birthday

On the occasion of your twentieth birthday congratulations and best wishes from your Papa
The birthday was on 2 May 1918. The telegram was not delivered until 5 May.

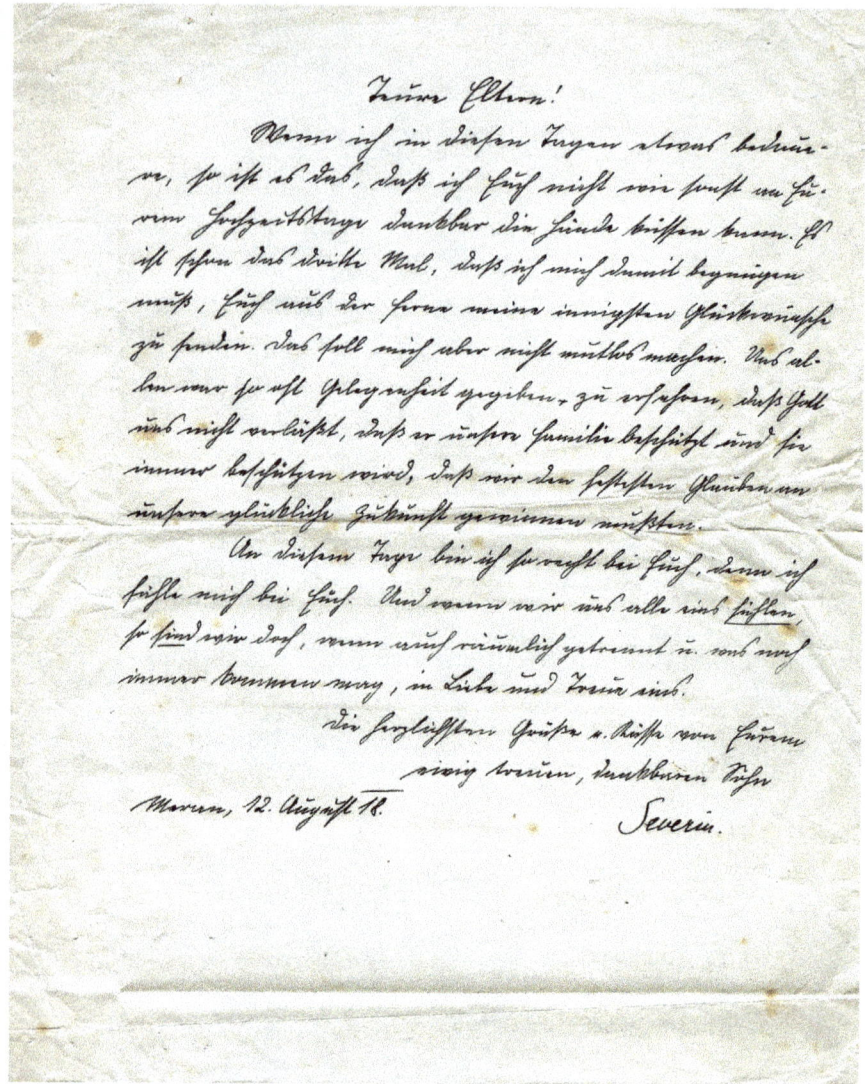

Letter to Severin's parents on the occasion of their wedding anniversary, August 1918

Letter to parents on occasion of their wedding anniversary

Dearest Parents!

If I regret anything these days, it is that on your wedding anniversary I cannot kiss your hands to show you my gratitude. This is now the third time that I have to be content with sending you my most heartfelt congratulations from afar.

That doesn't make me despondent, however. We have all so often had the opportunity to learn that God does not abandon us, that he protects our family and will always protect us, so that we must hold fast to the firmest belief in our happy future.

On this day I am so close to you that I feel I am with you. And if we all *feel* as one, then we will *be* as one, even if we are physically separated and whatever may come to us, unified in love and devotion.

Warmest greetings and kisses from your ever true and grateful son

Severin

Merano, 12 August 1918

[He was in the officers' convalescence home having had typhus. The parents' wedding anniversary was 15 August.]

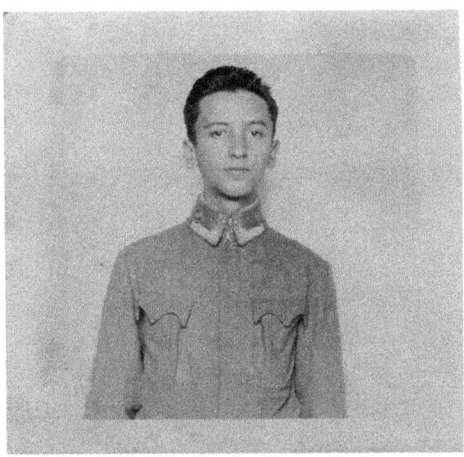

Undated

Certificate of Attendance on a Course
Wohlg. Herrn K.u.K. Faehnrich i. d. [?] S B, Instruction course in ….
Wilfersdorf [Austria] 25/6/1918

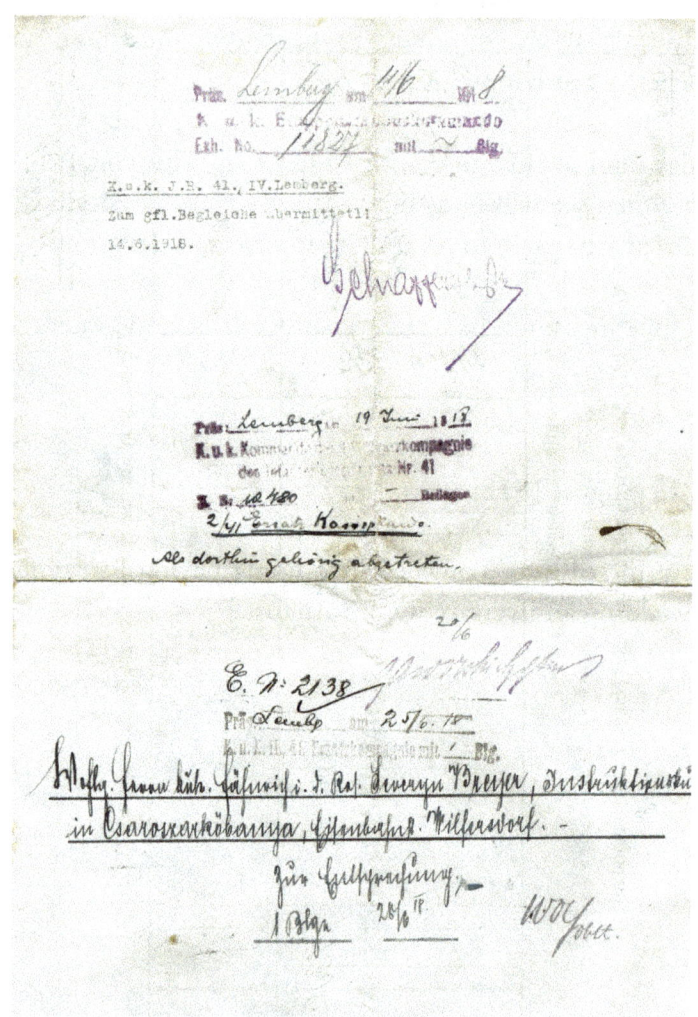

Certificate of attendance on a course

DIARY 2 covers the period from 18 September 1918 to 20 September 2019, including his engagement in the battles in the Val Frenzela in the Asiago region, his capture by the Italians at the end of the war and his 11-month detention as a prisoner of war in Mola di Bari.

Severin's family with space left for the absent son. L to R: Lotte, Walter, Ernestine (Mama), Simon (Papa; also in uniform), Franz

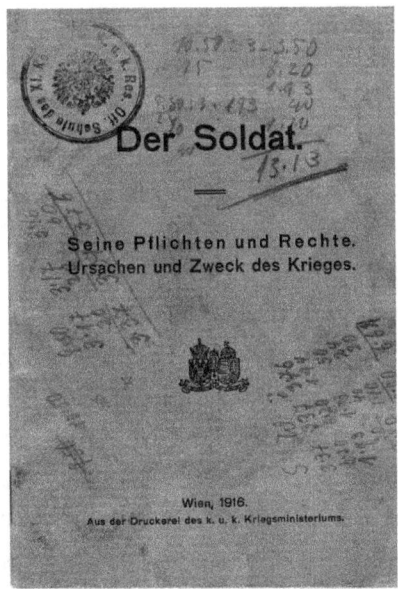

Der Soldat. The Soldier. His Duties and Rights. Causes and Purpose of War

Advice from *Der Soldat* on falling into enemy hands as a prisoner of war

It would be a great misfortune for the brave soldier to fall into enemy hands and become a prisoner of war. The dire conditions and privations that await him in that situation are greater than any in the field. Rough and inhuman treatment will be mostly meted out to him, and insidious illnesses carry off thousands of soldiers. Far from home and unknown, he will lie somewhere in foreign soil and there will be no loving hand to adorn his grave with flowers. Certainly a painful thought for all his loved ones.

But it can happen that even the bravest soldier is taken prisoner. In this case too, he must always be mindful of the sacred oath he has sworn. He must not answer any questions put to him that could be to the detriment of his comrades or his country. This would be a villainous treachery and treachery is despised even by the enemy. Even cruel threats, such as of death by shooting, should not under any circumstances persuade him to make any disclosures. He will only gain the respect of the enemy by steadfast silence.

Even in captivity, the soldier owes respect and obedience to his commanders and superiors. The soldier remains under all circumstances a soldier.

Soldiers who came into captivity unwounded must give an account of themselves once they return. This responsibility will fall lightly upon soldiers who were innocent prisoners. Sterner punishments and legal penalties will be meted out to a soldier who could be shown to have borne the blame for being taken captive. He and his whole family will suffer gravely as a consequence. So it is better to fall in honourable battle for emperor, king and country than to fall into ignominious captivity.

Obtaining information about the strength of the army, about its structure and disposition and its intentions is of great importance. If the enemy cannot gain such information from the prisoners – and **no prisoner must give it away** – he will try to obtain it by other means, for example by deploying spies.

These people endeavour by cunning means to infiltrate our lines and to get behind them, presenting themselves dressed as traders, coachmen, peasants or even often in the uniform of our own troops. They approach gullible soldiers and pose careful and seemingly quite harmless questions, from the answers to which they can draw important conclusions. The soldier must therefore always be reticent and mistrustful in dealing with such people whom he does not know. If something strikes him as suspicious, it is his duty to pass on this information to his senior officer, the nearest command or the nearest guard-house, constabulary or police post, so that the suspect can immediately be apprehended.

Your officers are your leaders in battle. They are the ones who look out for your needs. They are always considerate of and anxious to serve your welfare and to improve your situation as far as possible. You owe them your thanks, your love, your trust and your unquestioning obedience.

A fighting force without officers is leaderless and lost. **Soldiers! Always follow your officers with complete trust. Protect and honour them!**

Behaviour in battle
"The brave soldier does not recognise a flank or a rear; he knows only a front – and that is where the enemy is."

These words of an enemy general must always be kept at the forefront of Austro-Hungarian fighters' minds, as they contain great truth.

Once returned to Vienna, it is believed that Severin attended the Hochschule für Welthandel (World Trade University) in Vienna, possibly for a year, before enrolling in the University of Vienna, Juridical Department, where he studied part-time from 1920 to 1925, graduating with a doctorate in political science. His dissertation was entitled 'Towards a theory of assimilation'.

Enrolment booklet University of Vienna

Pages from University enrolment booklet. Some of Severin's lecturers were or later became very famous, notably Hans Kelsen, author of *The Pure Theory of Law*, and Othmar Spann, author of *Types of Economic Theory*.

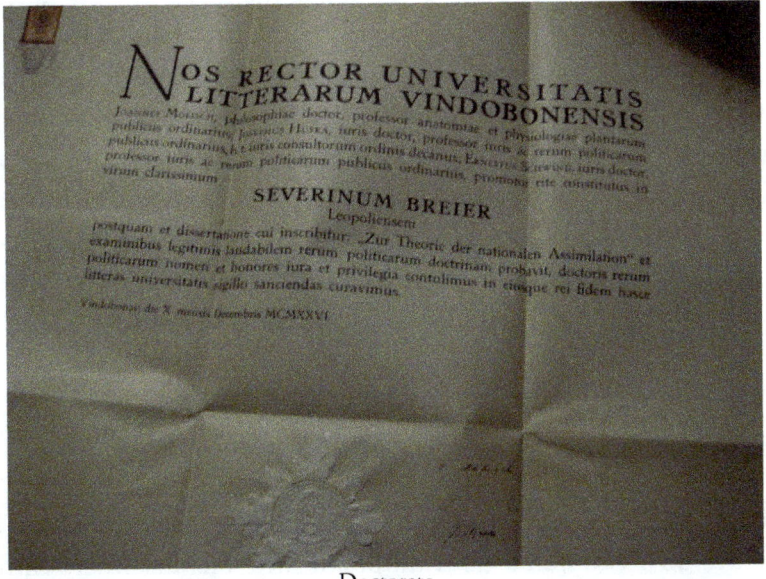

Doctorate

The family in the late 1920s. Back row: Walter, Ernestine (mother), Jani Ambrus (husband of Lotte), Franz. Front row: Severin, Lotte, Simon (Salomon, father)

Severin then worked in the international trade sections of banks in Vienna, with a spell in Berlin between 1929 and 1930.

In 1932 he met Annette Philipp (b. in Vienna in 1912) at a dance (to which her mother had encouraged her, somewhat reluctantly, to go). He pursued her single-mindedly until she eventually consented to marry him – tiring, she said, of being constantly asked! Annette was a governess to the children, barely younger than herself, of a wealthy family named Edelstein, who lived in a grand house on the Ring in Vienna. Severin and Annette married in May 1934, the day after his 36th birthday; she was at the time only 22. They lived at 99 Mariahilferstrasse, now Vienna's main shopping street.

In 1937, Severin's mother died, and it seemed to behove Severin to take on her business.

In March 1938, Adolf Hitler annexed Austria to the German Third Reich and on 15 March rode triumphant into Vienna, where Annette witnessed the rapturous crowds greeting him. In those early days of Nazi rule, Jews were not being rounded up but were permitted to leave Austria. Severin and Annette received such a dispensation and fleeing Austria was certainly a possibility for which they were in many ways prepared. The day came when Severin was summoned to attend a police station the following day. It was clear that this would not be to convey good news; so Severin and Annette fled during the night, taking the train first for Italy, where they spent a few weeks, before making their way via Switzerland to England. Meanwhile, when Severin failed to present himself to the police, his father, Simon, was called in. Simon purported not to know Severin's whereabouts, made a fuss, got angry and was let go. Undoubtedly, had this happened later in the Nazi era, Simon would have been sent to a concentration camp.

> Severin's brother **Franz** had married Stella Loewenberg in 1931 and in 1937 moved the family, which now included their son Peter (b. 1935) to Prague, where Franz was manager of the Czech branch of the Compass Verlag, the business publisher for whom he had worked in Vienna. The family emigrated to the USA in late February 1940, having obtained affidavits and visas at the last minute. One month after they left, all Jewish males in Prague were arrested – with consequences now known to all. Other than one trunk of personal items and eight US dollars that Franz was allowed to take out of the Reich, they had nothing. Like many other refugees, Franz took various menial jobs, rising to office manager at a factory in Chicago. The family moved to Little Rock, Arkansas, in 1952, where he took the position of controller and finally general manager at All States Trailer Co., a manufacturer of mobile homes.
> Franz and Stella's son Peter still lives in the USA.

Severin and Annette arrived in England in August 1938, having left the business and most of their belongings behind, and immediately set about bringing to England Annette's mother and sister, Renee, who soon joined them in Richmond, a suburb of London.

There is a story, possibly true, about the origins of the family connection with Australia, to which Severin and Annette moved in March 1939. Annette also had a brother called

> Severin's younger brother **Walter** studied music at the Universität für Musik und darstellende Kunst – Wien, from which he graduated summa cum laude. His main instrument was the double bass but he was also a brilliant piano player, including jazz. When the Nazis came to power and started to expel Jewish musicians from the various orchestras, Bronislaw Huberman (1882–1947), one of the most celebrated violinists of his time, decided to choose the most outstanding Jewish musicians in Europe, mainly from Austria, Poland and Hungary, and establish a symphony orchestra in Israel (then Palestine). In this way, as it later turned out, Huberman saved many lives. In 1936, the Palestine Symphony Orchestra (later Israeli Philharmonic Orchestra) was founded. Walter was one of the founders. At the age of 28, he was one of the youngest members of the Orchestra, and he played with the orchestra from the first concert in December 1936 in Tel Aviv until his death in October 1958.
>
> The Orchestra saved not only Walter but also his father, **Simon Breier**, by bringing him to Palestine a few years later, just in time. Simon died in Israel shortly after the war.
>
> During the first years, the musicians were not very well paid, and in order to make ends meet many of them, including Walter, gave music lessons and played also in cafés, bars and hotels. Walter was also one of the founders of the Tel Aviv Conservatory of Music.
>
> In 1941, in Tel Aviv, Walter married Lea/Lotte Goldszer (pronounced Goldscher), who was born in Berlin in 1920 and had fled with her parents to Palestine in 1938. They had two daughters, Esti (b. 1946) and Miri (b. 1950), both of whom still live in Israel.

Walter, who was a small-time importer–exporter. He is assumed to have wanted to go to Australia because it offered a safe haven for Jews.

On his application to immigrate, there was a question about his profession. Walter translated the word 'Unternehmer' (= entrepreneur) literally from German as 'undertaker'. Australia was short of undertakers, so they let him in …

One day, Walter met someone in a lift and got talking: this person turned out to be able to offer Severin a job as an overseer in a factory in Melbourne. It was the Breiers' deep wish, having escaped from Nazi Europe, to be anywhere, as long as they were safe and the family was together. Hence, they travelled to Australia, and Severin took up the job for a salary of some £A400 per year. Later, he moved on to set up his own import–export business for dolls, dolls' clothing and other toys.

> Severin's sister, **Lotte**, had been divorced by mutual agreement from her husband, Dr. Jani Ambrus, but afterwards Jani had regretted this and pestered her to live with him again. She did not want to, but promised that they would leave Vienna together and then finally separate. Three times, they paid money to a so-called Palestine Transport fund, to be smuggled into Yugoslavia, from where it was thought that there was a better chance of getting to Palestine. Twice they were swindled. Once, they got as far as Villach but then had to return to Vienna before trying again. Finally Lotte paid 600 Marks each for herself and Jani to be taken from Graz to Zagreb (then known as Agram). Lotte was impatient to leave and they finally departed Vienna on 9 January 1941. It appears that they had a quarrel on the street in Zagreb. In Yugoslavia, emigrants from elsewhere were tolerated and not notified to the police unless they came to public attention, in which case they would immediately be arrested by a secret detective. This was Lotte and Jani's fate. It is not known precisely what happened to them afterwards, except that they became two of the millions who perished in concentration camps.
> The International Red Cross, which was able to find people who went missing during the war and in some cases reunite families, was asked to trace Lotte but came up with nothing.

> Lotte is remembered with a page in the archive of Holocaust victims at Yad Vashem in Jerusalem, a page completed by Severin in 1971, stating her assumed place of death as Yugoslavia.

Safe in Australia the family may have been, but together they were not. Annette spent the entire period of WWII pleading with the Australian government to admit her mother and sister. The plea was repeatedly refused, on the grounds that all the ships were needed to transport troops. In March 1946, Annette's mother died of cancer in London, having been nursed through her illness by Renee. In January 1947, Renee contracted TB and died, aged only 33. Annette was heartbroken.

On a quirky note, it may be recorded that Walter kept the name Breier, while Franz changed it to Brier and Severin to Briar, the latter two in the interests of retaining the approximate pronunciation amid English-speakers.

Severin and Annette had two daughters, Beatrice (b. 1941) and Ingrid (b. 1945; the editor of this book).

Severin pursued his business, first in Melbourne and then in Sydney, to which the family moved in 1954. For a time, he employed a secretary/assistant, who happened to live in the block of flats next door. When times were leaner, he did everything himself, including acting as his own travelling salesman. Both daughters worked for him during their school and university holidays.

In the mid-1950s, Severin had surgery to remove gallstones. He was not completely cured, as it was realised that he had stones in the bile duct, which had not been removed. However, he returned to moderate health.

In 1958, a further tragedy struck. Walter fell ill with cancer. Severin decided not to travel to Israel to visit him – they had not met since before the war – for two reasons: one, in those days, travel was prohibitively expensive; two, he did not want to appear before his brother and, as it were, announce that his brother was dying. While Walter was fading, Severin's other brother, Franz, died suddenly in Arkansas of a heart attack. A scheme was hatched, in which the news of Franz's death would be kept from Walter, for whom the shock and grief would surely be too much to bear. Franz's son, Peter, then aged only 21, kept writing letters to Walter pretending to be Franz – a noble and difficult task. When Walter died, only 10 weeks after Franz, he still did not know that his brother had predeceased him. Walter was 50, Franz 54 when they died. Severin, the oldest sibling, now aged 60, was left alone.

As the family letters in the archive show, Severin's family was loving, caring and intensely appreciative of one another. How grievous, then, for Severin to lose both his brothers within such a short time. He bore the sorrow with as much stoicism as he could muster, but was deeply affected.

Although the Briars had settled and become naturalised in Australia and made a number of friends, mostly Jewish emigrants and refugees like themselves, they nevertheless hankered to return to Europe for a visit. Plans were made, money was saved. It so happened that Beatrice graduated from the University of Sydney and Ingrid left Sydney Girls' High School in the same year, 1961. This allowed the family to take time off and go on a world tour in 1962. They travelled by ship as far as Naples, where they disembarked. Beatrice and Ingrid went skiing in Switzerland, while Severin and Annette embarked on a tour of Europe.

They found Vienna much changed. Once it had been the 'gay' (in the original sense) city of culture and vibrancy, qualities lent to it by its large Jewish population. Now the Jews had almost all gone and the city seemed to be inhabited by resentful, self-pitying philistines. Annette, being blonde and blue-eyed, did not look Jewish; thus, many Viennese felt free to say to her, as if she were one of them, 'Wir haben ja so viel mitgemacht' [We suffered so much]. Yes, she would answer, so did we, actually .... It should be remembered that Vienna was a city in which the Jews were abused and humiliated more than almost anywhere else. One of the dreadful fates that Severin had escaped was cleaning slogans off the streets with toothbrushes dipped in acid, which Viennese Jews were forced to do during the war.

In 1962, Annette confirmed her wish to leave Australia and go to live in the UK. Ingrid ultimately felt likewise. Beatrice had stayed behind at the end of the 'world tour' and had married an Englishman and settled in London. There followed three years back in Australia for Severin, Annette and Ingrid while Ingrid attended the University of Sydney. Then it was emigration. Ingrid went first, arriving in London in February 1966, followed by Severin and Annette, who arrived in May of that year. By then Severin was already 68 years old, but he uprooted himself largely for the sake of his wife and daughter and continued to work as an importer and wholesaler, supplying to large retailers such as Harrods and Hamleys. He and Annette also bought two properties in different parts of London, each of which was converted into two flats, and these, rented out, became a good source of income.

Photos from the middle years. Top: Severin, Annette, Beatrice, Ingrid on Port Philip Bay, Melbourne, c. 1952. Bottom: Severin, Ingrid, Annette, Sydney, 1966

Although Severin had become a businessman, he continued to exercise his formidable intellect, making and managing investments, keeping up with the news and current affairs, reading in Italian (which he had taught himself in the POW camp), taking a course in the history of art and attending concerts and theatre, with or without Annette. Holidays to the Continent became frequent.

By the late 1970s, both Severin and Annette had compromised health, in Severin's case ischaemia and type 2 diabetes, though this was largely controllable by diet.

Last photo of Severin. Wedding of Ayesha and Michael Landesmann (son of Bobby Landesmann, Annette's cousin), Severin 2nd from right, Annette 4th from right. August 1981, Cambridge

In 1981, of which extracts of DIARY 3 are presented here, the Briars went on holiday to northern Italy, basing themselves in Merano. Severin had a yen to visit the area where he had served during WWI. The pair did the usual holiday activities, taking excursions to nearby towns and interesting buildings, borrowing books from the town library and finding and rating the best coffee shops in town. As frequently during his life, Severin kept a diary of the holiday, written in the old Gabelsberger shorthand, as before.

On 24 October, he wrote that he planned to visit the Vinschgau Valley the following day. This was apparently a very beautiful valley at the railhead, about which he had heard or which he had indeed visited during WWI. He already had slight 'chest congestion' when he undertook this excursion by train. He came back ill. Three days later, on 27 October, he suffered heart failure, which brought on pulmonary oedema. He was taken to hospital in Merano, where Annette accompanied him. Trying to reassure him, she said, 'You'll be all right'. In English, the lifelong sceptic, always bound to reality and the evidence, said 'I doubt it'. These were his last words. Annette travelled back from Italy three days later, accompanying Severin's body.

Annette was inconsolable over his loss, saying 'I have lost my life'. To some extent, she gathered her forces again, but died herself on a holiday in (then) East Germany in June 1985. Their ashes were mixed together and are in an urn in Ingrid's garden, on which is engraved their names and 'Endlich vereint, unendlich geliebt' [Together at last, endlessly loved].

Severin and Annette were both hoarders of documents of significance to themselves and eventually to their descendants. After Annette died, this legacy passed to Beatrice and Ingrid, where it remained cherished but largely 'unprocessed' until now.

The Beginning of WW1

On 28 July 1914, one month to the day after Archduke Franz Ferdinand of Austria and his wife were killed by a Serbian nationalist in Sarajevo, Austria-Hungary declared war on Serbia, effectively beginning the First World War.

Threatened by Serbian ambition in the tumultuous Balkans region, Austria-Hungary determined that the proper response to the assassinations was to prepare for a possible military invasion of Serbia. After securing the unconditional support of its powerful ally, Germany, Austria-Hungary presented Serbia with a rigid ultimatum on 23 July 1914, demanding, among other things, that all anti-Austrian propaganda within Serbia be suppressed and that Austria-Hungary be allowed to conduct its own investigation into the archduke's killing. Though Serbia effectively accepted all of Austria's demands except for one, the Austrian government broke diplomatic relations with Serbia on 25 July and proceeded with military preparedness measures. Meanwhile, alerted to the impending crisis, Russia – Serbia's powerful supporter in the Balkans – began its own initial steps towards military mobilization against Austria.

In the days following the Austrian break in relations with Serbia, the rest of Europe, including Russia's allies, Britain and France, looked on with trepidation, fearing the imminent outbreak of a Balkans conflict that, if entered into by Russia, threatened to explode into a general European war. The British Foreign Office lobbied its counterparts in Berlin, Paris and Rome with the idea of an international convention aimed at moderating the conflict; the German government, however, was set against this notion, and advised Vienna to go ahead with its plans.

On 28 July 1914, after a decision reached conclusively the day before in response to pressure from Germany for quick action – apart from

Kaiser Wilhelm II, who, according to some, still saw the possibility of a peaceful diplomatic resolution to the conflict, but was outmanoeuvred by the more hawkish military and governmental leadership of Germany – Austria-Hungary declared war on Serbia. In response, Russia formally ordered mobilization in the four military districts facing Galicia, its common front with the Austro-Hungarian Empire. That night, Austrian artillery divisions initiated a brief, ineffectual bombardment of Belgrade across the Danube River.

"[e]verything tends towards catastrophe and collapse," wrote British naval officer Winston Churchill to his wife at midnight on 29 July. He was proven right over the next several days. On 1 August, after its demands for Russia to halt mobilization met with defiance, Germany declared war on Russia. Russia's ally, France, ordered its own general mobilization that same day, and on 3 August, France and Germany declared war on each other. The German army's planned invasion of neutral Belgium, announced on 4 August, prompted Britain to declare war on Germany. Thus, in the summer of 1914, the major powers in the Western world – with the exception of the United States and Italy, both of which declared their neutrality, at least for the time being – flung themselves headlong into what became World War 1.

Source: https://www.history.com/this-day-in-history/austria-hungary-declares-war-on-serbia

DIARY 1

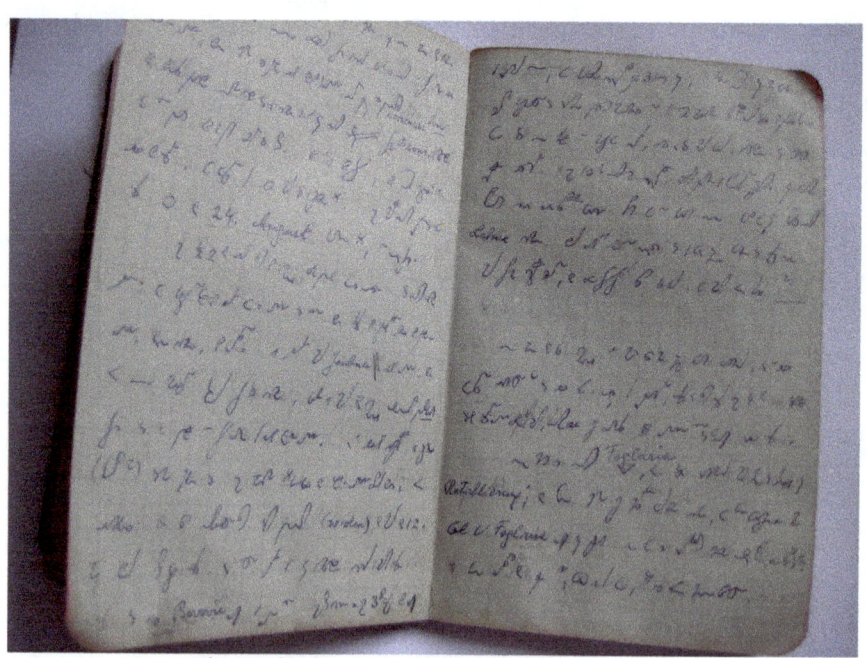

The notebook containing Diary I and sample pages

Editor's note:
Diary 1 was, like Diaries 2 and 3, originally written in Gabelsberger shorthand. However, unlike those later diaries, this one was transcribed by Severin himself in 1979, two years before he died. I have translated it into English. The first section below is his commentary on the diary. In the diary itself, there are some comments in square brackets; these, apart from the ones relating to place names, are mostly from Severin. 'I' in parentheses is Severin.

Italian Front 1917

The following report is a literal transcription of the diary I kept in 1917. Recently I went over in pen the pencilled – and thus in part only barely legible – shorthand notes I had made at that time in a notebook (with blue cover). My present comments on the notes are to be found either within square brackets in the text or at the foot of the relevant page.

As with my travel accounts since 1962, the notes of 1917 were devoid of style and their brevity made them fit only to recreate the experiences before *my* inner eye. A good description of the landscape and of the battles that took place at that time (the 11th Battle of the Isonzo) is given in *Der Kleine Beckmann* (which is in our possession), Vol. I, pp. 1064 and 1066, the passages marked.

From *Der Kleine Beckmann: Illustriertes Konversationslexicon für Schule und Haus*, 2nd improved edition. Leipzig and Vienna: Verlagsanstalt Otto Beckmann, 1928, pp. 1064–66. (Trans. IC)

p. 1064: In order to understand the following events, it is necessary to construct an image of the field of action on which they took place. This is the most desolate, soulless part of the whole Isonzo front – the bleakest tract of Alpine karst with just here and there patches of pitiful

vegetation. Hill follows hill, each more dreary than the last, most bearing no other designation than that given them by the surveyor – spot height 208, spot height 235. A few miserable villages cling to them, long since fallen into miserable ruins. Nowhere is there any shade, even a little coolness. Everywhere unyielding, hostile stone, which the southern sun turns red-hot.
[The area mentioned is bordered approximately by Villach in the north and Gorizia in the south.]

p. 1066: For his 11th Isonzo strike, Cadorna chose the moment of Haig's army's mighty onslaught against the submarine base. He had put 6,500 guns in place, which began firing in the afternoon of 17 August (see map). Next to the karst plateau on the southern flank, the 3rd Army under the Duke of Aosta stood at the ready, and from the Wippach [now Vipava] to the Krn [mountain], the 2nd Army under General Capello. The Colonel General Boroevic kept the main forces of his army gathered on the southern front section, as he was expecting the strongest push from the enemy to come over the karst and through the hollow of the Wippach. On the 19th, the mass assault by the Italians began along the whole 80 km-wide front from Mrzli Vrh# to the sea. The main attack from the Italian 2nd army was directed towards the Heiligengcist plateau, attackers and defenders both digging in in a furious to and fro. Ever more numerous enemy reserves crossed the Isonzo near Canale [Kanal ob Soči], spread out and stormed towards the slopes. During the night of 23/24 August, Monte Santo had to be abandoned, but Monte Gabriele was held fast in an iron grip. Everybody knew that the Gabriele was the key to the whole position, right up to the Wippach. The Austrian Major Alexander Huebner, who lost an arm, described this long drawn-out battle for this terrible mountain: "On 1 and 2 September as well, the fighting raged with undiminished ferocity. According to the accounts of prisoners, three Italian regiments were fighting across Veliki Hrb, the northernmost sub-peak of Monte Gabriele, more than a thousand paces wide. With fierce counterattacks, we tried to win back the ground that had been snatched away from us. Nevertheless, the Italians broke through on 4

September. At 7.45am, they were on the summit of Gabriele. The brigadier ordered all available forces on to the mountain. At 8.30 in the morning, we could see that the Italians were trying to set up positions on the brow of Gabriele. A barrage struck all around the mountain. We were doing it so that the Italians wouldn't bring up reinforcements and the *Italians* were doing it so that we wouldn't. A wall of flames glowed around Gabriele. The fighters were cut off from the world. The mountain no longer belonged to the earth: hell had taken possession of it. By midday we noticed some Italians on the slope facing us. At 1.22pm, our heroes stormed forward. The enemy fled. At 1.25pm, the crest was ours. At 2.44pm it was back in Italian hands. At 3pm, our brave heroes launched a renewed attack and flung the enemy off the mountain. However, at 3.45pm, he renewed his advance and by 4.05pm he was at the top again. At 4.50pm, our infantry climbed up again. At 5.15pm, the enemy charged again, but in the evening we finally succeeded in holding the mountain. Survivors left to us included a major from the No. 13 Infantry Regiment, 14 officers and 100 men. Artillery fire raged throughout the night. Dust and smoke. At 11.15am, this quietened down. We could see our people on the Gabriele summit rushing back and forth. However, at midday, an Italian battalion attacked. At 1.48pm, they fled in retreat. Our artillery fired after them. At 2.30pm, the enemy tried once again to advance. Our fire pinned them down. Yet, at 3.50pm, they stormed forward en masse, but were beaten back. At 6.55pm, the Italians launched an attack from the saddle of the Dol to St Katharina [photo attached, source Österreichische Nationalbibliothek/Austrian National Library*]. We beat him back. The Italians had suffered such losses that they discontinued any further attacks for the time being."

The bloody struggle went on along the whole front, the Italians ceaselessly throwing more reserves in. At most, eight battalions of reserves followed each battalion in the front line; if the first line of attackers was cut down, a new line would automatically move up from behind. The Italian 2nd Army, in the centre of the battle front, gained an area on the Heiligengeist plateau near the Chiapovano [Čepovan, western Slovenia] valley, believed they had made a breakthrough, and their leadership hoped they could turn the enemy's flank to the south. Counterattacks finally held the assault in check, which had, along a 28-km stretch, advanced 7km deep into the territory and won it.

However, the progress of the 3rd Army on the south flank seemed more significant: it was on Hermada [Mt Ermada, Slovenia**], supported from the sea by fire from English and French warships that had come within 5km of Trieste. But from there they could go no further. In mid-September, the colossal battle dissolved into a few partial attacks, the fighting men being by now completely exhausted. Cadorna had put 50 divisions into this decisive battle; their numbers had been unimaginably thinned.

But the Austrian-Hungarian army was also so worn out that the leadership closed their minds to the fact that Trieste could no longer be defended against such an offensive. This problem awoke in the K.u.K. high command the realisation that a strong offensive mounted from the defensive position was necessary to counter the threat most effectively. But it was patently clear that such a counterattack on a grand scale could not be mounted without the collaboration of German troops. However, since the beginning of the war with Italy, every request for support had been turned down with the observation that this war was inherently deeply rooted in the popular instinct and hence it was the business of the Habsburg monarchy and it was without question up to them to fight it out alone. Now such resistance had been allowed to drop and a joint strike to roll back the Isonzo front from the north towards the previous breakthrough at Tolmein [Tolmin, northwestern Slovenia] was being considered. Although Ludendorff would have preferred to completely crush Romania through an energetic offensive from the Moldau [Vltava river], he agreed to the plan after consultation with Hindenburg and Emperor Wilhelm. General Otto v. Below with Lt-General Kraft v. Delmensingen as his chief of staff were designated as leaders of the German 14th Army forces to be sent into action at the

Isonzo. The German high command put seven divisions into place who, strengthened by the K.u.K. troops, were to mount the main push.

#The Mrzli vrh was a hard-fought 'bare hill'.
* Also from https://picryl.com/media/blick-gegen-dol-sattel-vsvka tharina27817-7b0c56: The Isonzo Front was one of the First World War's most brutal campaigns: 29 months of trench warfare, and 12 major battles leading to more than 500,000 casualties including 200,000 Austro-Hungarian troops. Italian death toll was awful: 300,000 of half of the entire Italian losses in the First World War were along this 90km stretch. Thousands of Slovenian civilians from the Goriza and Gradisca region died from malnutrition in Italian refugee camps during the campaign. Stretches of fortifications have been restored and a 'Walk of Peace' has been created threading through the truly beautiful Slovenian landscape linking sites of unimaginable suffering.
** From https://www.turismofvg.it/en/108479/open-air-museum-of-mt-ermada: The sinkholes, the passages between the rocks and the natural caves of the Karst Plateau perfectly adapted to the needs of the Great War. Trenches, observation posts and housing for soldiers were built in no time, practically creating an insurmountable barrier for the Italians.

At the beginning of the diary are some dates, the officer school graduates assigned to the (16) Trained Replacement Company of the (41.) Infantry Regiment and a list of all the people with whom I had resolved to maintain correspondence. The dates are:

1916

8.5	Left Vienna
11.5	Reported for duty [in Lemberg, now Lviv]
13.5-17.6	Quarantine in Szatmar-Ne'meti [now Satumare, Romania]
20-24.6	In Pohulanka Barracks [Lemberg]
24.6	Admission to military service with III Replacement Company I. R. [Infantry Regiment] 41
28.8	Recognition of the One-Year Volunteer Law
4-11.9	Holiday in Vienna
2.10	Volunteer medical examination with I. R. 41
6.12.1916-13.2.1917	Officer School in Jägerndorf [now Krnov, Silesia]
28.12.1916-2.1.1917	Christmas leave

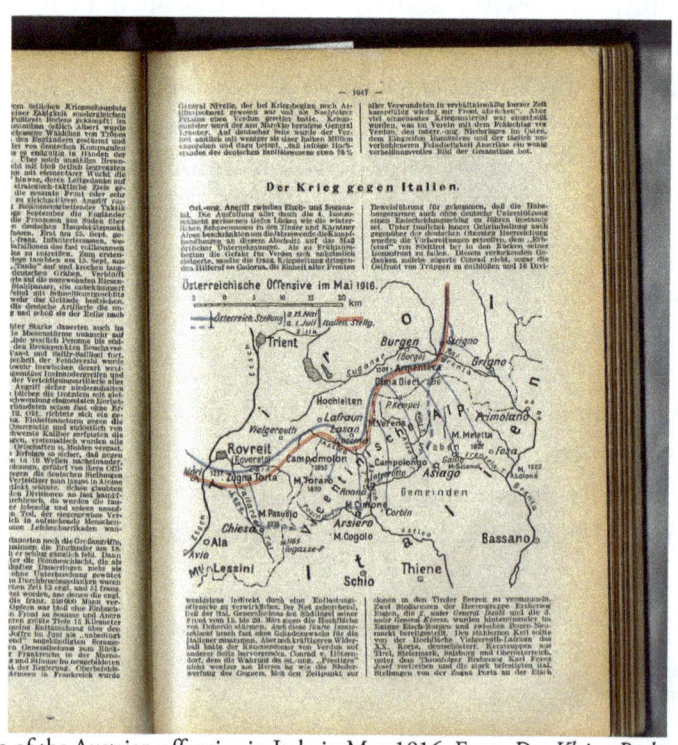

Map of the Austrian offensive in Italy in May 1916. From *Der Kleine Beckmann*

"To my dearly beloved Mama from your loyal son Severin. Jägerndorf [Krnov, Czech Republic, just within border, very near border with Poland] 4/II/1917."

1917

16-24.2	One-Year Volunteer Division
28.2-21.5	Trained Replacement Company II/28th
23.3	Departure from Lemberg
25.3	Short reunion with my dear ones
26.3-21.5	In Vodice [formerly Woditz, Croatia] near Stein [c. 12 km N of Ljubljana]
17/18.5	With the Company in Laibach [Ljubljana]
22.5-30.7	On officer training course of 3rd Corps in Peteline [?] near St Peter [Sv. Petar, south of Vodice] [i.e. further officer training]
	Beginning of June and 10.6 Air raids [enemy]
24-30.6	War bonds subscription leave in Vienna
12.7	Excursion with the school to the Adelsberg Grotto (Postojna, Slovenia), mine-thrower section in Mautersdorf [Matenja vas, south of Postojna], radio station Rakitnik [south of Postojna]

23/24.7 7th	Flying Post Divazza [Divača, c. 15-20 km ENE of Trieste], Trieste [air attack there]; Miramare [c. 7-8 km along coast to the north of Trieste], swimming in the sea
2.8	Air raid in Čepovan [Slovenia, c. 20 km north of Trieste], bombing nearby
3.8	Assigned to the 10th/41st Field Company. Beginning of service at the front in 1C-Line
17.8	Beginning of the 11th Battle of the Isonzo
19.8	First engagement
23/24.8	Second engagement – evacuation of Monte Santo and retreat to Foglaria
1.9	Promotion to (Acting) Platoon Leader of the One-Year Volunteers
9.9	Silver medal for bravery conferred by order of the Regiment

Medal for bravery ("Der Tapferkeit") awarded to Severin Breier September 1917. The particular act of bravery was to run up a hill under fire to deliver a message to his commanding officer. The medal still in our possession is made of a base metal because of a shortage of silver during the war years. After the war, Severin received a silver medal, which unfortunately has been lost.

25.9	Departure for the field hospital at Haidenschaft [now Ajdovčina]
30.9	Departure for the reserve hospital in Laibach
4.10	Departure from there on hospital train
6.10-13.12	In military hospital in Grinzing [suburb of Vienna]

Field hospital in Grinzing, Vienna, main street, where Severin was ill in 1918, with anaemia following dysentery

14.12.1917-7.1.1918	'Agricultural' leave
20-28.12.1917	In Kattowitz [Katowice, Poland] and Dabrowa [Dąbrowa Górnicza, near Katowice] [with father]

1918

6/7.1	In Bielitz [Bielsko-Biała, south of Katowice], Heinzendorf [Hynčice, c. 30km south of Ostrava], Ernsdorf [Jaworze, c. 5 km south west of Bielsko-Biala]
9.1	Reported for duty with Regimental Officer staff
12.1	To IV/41st Replacement Company
31.1-6.2	Seven days' solitary confinement [for breach of detention in barracks].

THE DIARY
Covers 1 August to 14 October 1917

1 August

A platoon leader from the 41st tells us that our division went into position yesterday evening. None of us felt particularly disheartened by that. Train from Assling [Jesenice, c. 60 km NNE of Trieste] to Podmelec [c. 60 km north of Trieste] travels through deep valleys; rugged, sunny mountain slopes to either side. A sequence constantly repeated: a babbling stream, a tunnel, a few small isolated houses with reddish light coming from them or with window frames gaping open … one can tell that the front is not far off. Arrived at the terminus Podmelec at 1 am, stayed in the compartment until 5 o'clock, since our transport officer cannot start anything during the night. At 6.30 we arrived at the Santa Lucia [Ladja Lucija] collection point and were given coffee; at 10 o'clock we are to march on. The streets are extremely busy here with all sorts of traffic – cars, lorries and people. Santa Lucia is often hit by enemy artillery, probably because there is a bridge here crossing a tributary of the Idria. We are all calm, not excited, almost nonchalant and nearly as cheerful as ever. We have not yet seen any active combat, after all, and we have many old battle-tried soldiers among us. Interrupted while writing by an air raid; it was meant for our particular valley, but our batteries let off such a barrage that the enemy was forced to retreat to the north and thus to vanish from view. Two vultures are circling, startled by the shots, high above the forest. Departure from S. Lucia for Čepovan. The march took us over a rough, steep path through the mountains and we had to put in quite an athletic performance with our heavy rucksacks. My first sacrifice was a two-volume Jules Verne, which I had unfortunately been lugging around with me. Other items will doubtless go the same way. As we approached Čepovan and came within hearing distance of the artillery fire, I felt a wave of relief to know that I was near the front and free of the endless number of columns, depots, batteries, etc. – not to be far from our goal. In Čepovan we got lunch at 5 o'clock. Like my pals, I ate my tinned food on the road; one soon gets used to the soldier's life.

2 August
We moved into tents for the night; I slept very well, in spite of heavy (short) rain in the night. Raided by an Italian squadron: small bombers surrounding the large aircraft that had to be defended. Recognisable by the large areas of colour and shapes. Quite a lot of bombs fell, mostly on the mountain slope opposite. Many (soldiers) ran for cover at the edge of the forest, others stayed put (probably the better course of action). The Russian prisoners of war ran too, one was killed; several wounded; two children are also said to have met their deaths in a fire started by a bomb.

3 August
Assigned to the 10th Field Company; although I am no longer among the closest of my friends, I am glad to be under Lt. Jenkner, who is a good man to be with. Dr. Landau (Officer School) and Cadet Nicolaus from the Trained Replacement Company and from the course are here too. Camped in tents again near our combat train.

4 August
Yesterday left our train at 3 o'clock and went by cart belonging to 9th Company to take up our positions together. The village of Britof [c. 20 km north of Ljublana] and the monastery on Monte Santo [10 km N of Gorizia] were just undergoing a heavy round of artillery fire at the time. Not pleasant being on the road after passing through Britof. At any rate two small 'cave shelters' offering shelter to 'poor travellers'. One of the carriage horses, on which I had rested my rucksack for a while, was hit by shell splinters; I had a feeling of satisfaction when we got to the position. Although one made slow progress with the rucksack, I found it easy to make the upward climb once the position was close at hand. Signboard reading 'to 10th/11th Field Company' showed me the right direction. Talked to Cadet Nicolaus until my fellow soldier of the Company arrived, then we two went to see the Company Commander, who greeted me with the words (which pleased me), "Oh, I know you already." Night in a cave shelter at Company Command. Slept well although there was work going on around me;

Italians left us completely alone. Afterwards reported to my train, number 2 (in the position). One quickly gets used to all this shooting – which of course is nothing compared with what is to come – it begins to seem a matter of course. The enemy batteries are just beginning to bring their firing line closer to our (C-)position; it may not be long before they start aiming direct into our trenches. Yesterday's bombardment at Monte Santo was – according to one of the observation officers – a 'dress rehearsal'; one man in our Regiment died, a mine fell directly on his head; shells [destroying it] at the entrance to a cave shelter wounded several, killed two, Lt. Tannenzapf, Commander of 11th Company, wounded. The artillery is starting to make one feel rather more anxious; shots and shells are hitting targets not far behind our position.

7 August

Two fairly quiet days. One also gets used to shells falling nearby and splinters flying past very close to one. Here I had to suffer something of which I had previously had only the vaguest notion, namely the rain; I was not prepared for it [how could one have been?] and so I, books, papers, rifle got duly wet.

As the opening in the wall near me is not rectangular but triangular [cross-section] and since moreover the earth above my head is very sparse, from time to time I get sand [earth] falling on my head – the more it rains, the more it comes down. Having learnt my lesson, I positioned my tent further down in the opening, so that the sand falls on the tent, where the rain turns it into mud – this doesn't matter, as long as I don't get it in my face. … It is getting boring; Dr. Landau and Gottesmann have lent me little books and newspapers; that helps; smoking helps too. Those on duty go to the position or to work; I am not [as One-Year Volunteer] being used for work, although my patrol leader would like to see it happen; the other men of different ranks, who now have to join in the work, scramble for the job of platoon inspection corporal [24 hours], so that they do not actually have to work, and so I come away empty-handed, which pleases me greatly, since I have the most blissful sleep, have the most beautiful and varied dreams and wake up in the morning feeling quite comfortable. The food could be better, and there should be more drinks and extras available [more than the essential food]. I get by with the amount of tobacco I have, though.

11 August

We are still living from day to day; if one has nothing to read for any length of time, it becomes unspeakably boring and gets on one's nerves. I spent the whole of last night working with two of my crowd to enlarge my shelter by the wall and to put in some corrugated iron. Now my 'dwelling' is at least passably fit for human habitation, cannot sit up in it though, but I can stretch my legs out and can accommodate my things comfortably; besides, I am protected from the rain. Yesterday I took over the newly formed 2nd troop of the 2nd Patrol. Among them were five who were assigned to the [Regiment no.] 94, all of them from the Reserve District Reichenberg [Sudetenland; Liberec, Czech Republic, c. 80 km NNE of Prague]; I am glad about this because of the language. This morning the Katzelmacher [troublemaker = Italian] allowed us a bit more peace, now to make up for it he is letting off his heavy shells and mines quite near to us.

A small air battle a short time ago. Both flyers used machine guns to shoot at each other. Ours turned tail pretty soon, probably having suffered some damage. In the last few days the Italian airmen have been coming over not in squadrons but one at a time, but all day long. Tonight I am on duty supervising work on the communications trench; I am looking forward to breaking out of this dreary idleness; oh, but if only I had something to read tomorrow!! As it is, the best thing is to snooze the time away.

13 August

Had platoon inspection last night. At about 11 o'clock the enemy fired on a group carrying wire barriers; he must have become aware of them somehow, probably they were making themselves a bit obvious. He was firing rifle grenades and mines, but also heavy and smaller shells; additionally there was some rifle fire from the infantry.

No appetite; having slept all night and well into the morning, I don't even feel like coffee or soup or bread today. Added to which is the calamitous [unavailable] water situation. Would gladly swap an equal quantity of coffee for some decent drinking water.

A new company sergeant, Mareinko, has taken over the company. He is a well-known sergeant-major in the Regiment. He was company sergeant in the 3rd Company when I was there. Prototype of a sergeant-major.

In the afternoon, some well-aimed hits in the immediate proximity of our position. In the morning in the latrine, the fragments of a grenade fell all around me. In the afternoon, a 50–60 cm-long fragment fell on the ground in front of me; I was just at that moment slowing my steps. If I had not been doing so, I could now be on the way to the divisional medical unit or even in a better hereafter.

It seems downright trivial to be writing this sort of thing, when I shall probably often encounter more dangerous situations in battle and shall not be able to describe them here.

The day before yesterday the foxhole [no second exit, as in the 'cave shelter'] which houses our Company Command received a direct hit: 1 dead, 1 badly wounded, 1 slightly wounded.

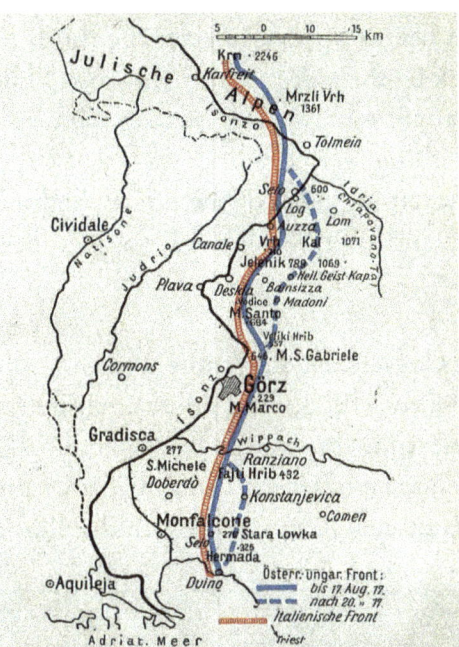

Map of the field of war against Italy, showing the Italian front (red line), the Austro-Hungarian front up to 17 August 1917 (solid blue line) and the Austro-Hungarian front after 20 August 1917 (dotted blue line). From *Der Kleine Beckmann*

17 August

This day is one of those that will remain forever in my memory [prior to the beginning of the 11th Battle of the Isonzo]. It began in a very extraordinary way: our two cadets and we two One-Year Volunteers went to make an inspection and critical survey of the cave shelters in the 1st and 2nd Lines. When we got back, a nice breakfast with the Lieutenant was ready for us. Stretched out on my bunk afterwards, even had something to read, expected that the day would pass with this agreeable method of killing time. At 10 o'clock the Italians shifted their fire nearer and direct at our lines; in the first instance scored only one direct hit. I heard someone shout 'ambulance' and hurried along with the ambulance people to the spot where the shout came from. Grenades (fairly small calibre) had blown in the wooden roof of a small shelter in which three people lay; those who had been assigned to me from Infantry Regiment 94 [see above].

Two of them had been ripped to pieces; the third, Prasser, wounded. At first I was struck by the pieces of the dead men's bodies and couldn't pay attention to anything else. The bits lay there as though this were the most natural thing in the world: two feet [legs] with gaiters, a behind with the adjoining parts of the upper thigh [and other pieces]. The flesh was soft and spongy; all the blood had been drained out of them.

I knew one of the Geislers, Rudolf, quite well and cannot conceive that such a fine and vigorous life should be extinguished. Until recently he occupied a place near me, but had to leave it and make do with a place in that shelter because an older man coming back from leave alleged he had a claim to this place. Otherwise he would still be alive.

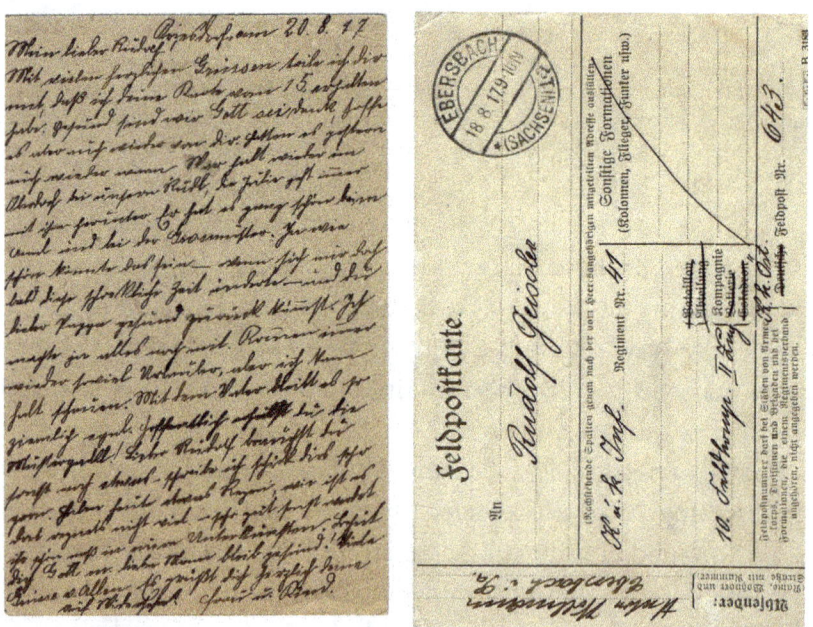

Postcards from Geisler's relatives that arrived after his death were kept among Severin's souvenirs

Looking at the wounded man and the remains of the two dead men, I was filled with a horror of death. Before this I had never had much sympathy with those who decide to settle their accounts with life [so to speak]; I thought this time was a sort of bad transitional period, which one normally survived ... and if not, it was just an exception and not to be reckoned with. In that moment too I had only one thought – the will to live.

11-12 o'clock fairly quiet, as though the enemy was giving us time to swallow our rations. When he let loose again, some of the fire was directed at our platoon and there was particular concentration on the machine gun platoon. Now it began to get serious; there was drumfire in the true sense of the word, ceaseless, round after round. If we had received a direct hit at the entrance to the cave shelter we would have been in trouble; it was unlikely, though. We remained sitting down until we couldn't any longer, stood up again to stretch our limbs. I read for as long as I was able, trying to get so absorbed in my reading as to forget temporarily where I was and what was happening.

Who knows what today may bring.

Shortly before 9 o'clock, the firing died down and I went outside to see if anything had happened. Next to the shelter that had been hit by the shell in the morning there was now a crater, deep and wide, caused by a heavy shell striking into loose earth; one had to get over the crater to reach the trench, which was now hardly recognisable; my place was intact. Many had remained in their places ... it is actually [almost] as safe in one of the traverse recesses as in the cave shelter, unless it receives a direct hit. Collected blanket and bread and went back to the cave shelter, where my platoon commander and I got ready to sleep.

While I am writing, someone sitting at the entrance has been hurt and bandaged and is going straight away to the emergency station. The Mojes [dialect word for Ukrainian peasants] are demonstrating their well-known briskness [ironic]; it takes only one shot for them all to vanish into the cave. The Romanians are said to be better than many others at decisive moments; when they see their superiors advancing, they follow without much hesitation.

18 August

And there was morning and there was evening ... a day. An endless day, whose hours stretched out to appalling length. At midday the entrance to the cave shelter was partly blocked as a result of shelling action. Inside my head I had a strong sensation of pressure, and I thought, 'That's it, now you've had it'; but it proved to be nothing; the platoon leader [illegible] suffered a burst left eardrum. We sat there until evening, with nothing to eat except perhaps a piece of bread, and black coffee with it, but with a raging thirst for water.

9 o'clock relief, in that the 2nd Platoon was ordered into the big Company cave shelter, which is the best constructed and the only totally secure one in the Regiment. My lieutenant generously let me share his meal, so that I got only some soup from the mess rations and slept through the rest. 'Time is money,' the lieutenant says. 'Who knows? We may be on the march in two hours' time.' I sincerely hope he is right.

Postcard to Franz Schwarz, who was killed in battle before this could reach him

19 August

It was dawn when I was woken by noise in the cave shelter. The Italians had attacked and occupied [captured] the positions of the 5th, 6th and 8th Companies. Our 2nd Platoon got orders to repair to the trench that we had been holding. Had hardly arrived when the order came, 'Forward', so forward we went; no reserves at our rear. We threw the Italians out of the B-Line and then consequently out of the A-Line. What I would say about the attack is: we ran forward and the attack went forward; if anyone hung back nobody normally said anything to him; only there is not much point in shirking in the midst of drumfire. At that time, our artillery was constantly in action and made a considerable contribution to our success. I went ahead quietly and quite fast, feeling more confident if the enemy artillery was not in action, just enemy machine guns. [With hindsight, my impression of the battle at the front is: we attack, they run; the others charge, we run – there is no hand-to-hand fighting.] Met Cadet Nicolaus in B-Line, had a little look round there; I felt almost like someone whose heart is full and who is minded to do someone a good turn. I got hold of a revolver there – not a standard issue Army revolver; ate two applies and had a word with the [= my] men. A bullet hit infantryman Schwarz there; it brought him an easy death on the spot; there was no sign of the injury to be seen on him; I pressed the lids down over his glassy eyes.

Suddenly it seemed to us that we were being bypassed on the left flank by the Italians, and we were undecided whether to run back or not; but it turned out to be our own men, and at that moment we were given the order to move forward and those who had run back had to turn on their heels again. As we advanced, I fell in with the 22nd Rifle Regiment and was fairly far ahead, so that I could experience the capture of Italian prisoners at first hand. It is not surprising that they show great cowardice when they are captured and act in a fawning manner. But they do not give the impression of being great heroes at any other time either. They are mostly young men of a similar type, not particularly strong, with thin moustaches. Many wounded, especially Italians, lay in the trenches, corpses too. My senses were so numbed that I strode over mutilated bodies and past seriously wounded men with no feeling of horror nor of pity. I occupied myself by picking up various things: an Italian gas mask, which a prisoner had just thrown away, rifle and machine gun cartridges, a rifle catch, an Italian bayonet, tins of rusks and of coffee (these however of Austrian origin). I ate a lemon while I was walking. I was very hot and, by the time the attack came to a halt, I was tired. I was in the midst of the riflemen, ran along the line looking for my own men, discovered on the way from the 5th Company that Lt. Jenkner was nearby. [Jenkner, very amiable, good-looking, respectable, late thirties, with smart Lehar-moustache; I have fond memories of him.] Found him soon afterwards with several people from the Company on a hillside, between B- and C-Lines; command of the 2nd Battalion was not far away. My fellow solider Schick from the 5th Company was there too and we spent the time from half past eleven until about half past six in the most awful drumfire [on open terrain!]. Advancing in the battle, as we did in the morning, was easy compared with the strain to which our nerves were subjected then. One doesn't feel this at the time, but today – 20 August – I was aware of the strain I must have been under, as I feel quite exhausted.

The terrain of the Battles of the Isonzo.
Source: blick-gegen-dol-sattel-vsvkatharina27817-7b0c56.jpg

The greater the frequency and proximity of hits from shells and mines, the more this certain nameless feeling impresses itself upon us; Jenkner found the right term for it, saying it was like a sixth sense; one is indifferent but at the same time intensely alert to personal danger; one talks about all kinds of things and philosophises and yet is sharply intent on remembering the lethal capabilities of each and every bullet that strikes home. Not far away, the enemy had chosen a position and covered it with rounds of shells; on the right, he was hurling his heaviest shells. Above us on the slope of the mountain and also in front of us there is the firing of mines; everywhere there is infantry fire. All around us trees had been stripped of their branches, trunks had been snapped, shrubs uprooted; the whole of nature suggested a barren wasteland. From time to time, earth poured over us. A small fragment (or stone?) caught me under the left eye and caused an insignificant injury.

One time when it was raining down heavily on us, the lieutenant asked if anyone was wounded, but everyone was all right. [I should here mention that the soldier – Company Orderly – mentioned in the following passage lay next to the lieutenant (because of his position as Company Orderly), with myself immediately next to them. I omitted to mention this in the diary. Since Jenkner was talking only to me, over the head of the soldier who lay between us, the latter suggested eventually – shortly before the following incident took place – that I should change places with him, so as to make it more convenient for Jenkner and me. Very probably, if this had not been the case, I should have been the one who was hit, for we were lying very close together, as I have said.] The next shower of earth was accompanied by a very strong blast and when it was over Jenkner called out, 'Bandages, quick!'. The Company Orderly had his left leg shot away immediately below the knee; the lower leg hung from a tiny strip of flesh like some foreign body that had been put there and did not belong, and blood flowed out like the source of a stream. I quickly pulled out my packet of bandages and bound up the leg below the knee. It took what seemed a long time for the emergency squad to come and take him away on a stretcher. [During the time described here, we were quenching our thirst with cooling water from the machine guns.] Jenkner had had enough by now; he went off to the cave shelter belonging to the Bayonet Command, and we went with him. It was relatively safe there, and hardly had we arrived when the artillery fire died down considerably. Jenkner shared a cold dinner with me and Schick there. [Jenkner was very amiable, good-looking, respectable, late thirties, with a smart Lehar-moustache; I have fond memories of him.]

A cave shelter. Source: WW1 shelter 9200291_bildarchivaustria_at_Preview_15605081.jpeg

A cave shelter. Source: WW1 shelter 9200291_bildarchivaustria_at_Preview_15453880.jpeg

The Company gathered together at the cave shelter. There were [only] 15–20 men [left], who then reached the Boroevic [or Borovič] Gorge at daybreak; I myself stayed behind with Lt. Runes who had been wounded in the right forearm [he had said to Jenkner, 'Please just leave me a One-Year man'] and also accompanied him to the hospital, where they also brush-treated my wound, which had become sticky with plaster.

20 August
In Boroevic Camp the entire Bayonet and 10th and 12th Companies in reserve.

Unquenchable thirst; living together at such close quarters and the temperature contribute to the problem. Tired and sleepy at night. Drew up a report for Jenkner, at his request, on my conduct and the situation as I saw it on the 19th. He wants it so as to be able to assess more accurately the performance of the officers and men and the general situation.

Like Napoleon, I could now sleep for 24 hours, far away from here, in a soft bed. I have hardly slept for the last three nights.

21 August

Today we shall have some more sleep and water to drink. My ears are a bit 'queer'. The drumfire has 'addled' my hearing (as we usually say). The 2nd Bayonets may well consist of only three companies at present. The 8th was virtually wiped out and taken prisoner. 8th and 12th are supposed to combine to form a new company, while the former 4th is to attach itself to the 2nd Bayonets. Thus, possible that we shall be going into positions again very soon.

22 August

… was another rest day, if one may call it that, for there was considerable firing from the enemy on the camp, and flyers came over constantly to reconnoitre. Artillery more intense, but still only a prelude.

23 August

Inscribed on my memory in letters of blood. Camp came under heavier fire, nerves were tensed. Jenkner came storming into our shelter in a state of agitation: 10th to sling rifles immediately and go up to the edge of the Boroevic Gorge (about 1 o'clock); inadequate cover; then advanced to the (?) trench. Trench mortars, those much-feared weapons of fire but having a greater effect on the morale than in practice. At 5 o'clock Jenkner sent me forward to a point where I could shoot from, so that, together with the 12th Company, we could ward off the enemy if he were to outflank us [a good part of the Company was supposed to follow me], but only a few men came after me, as it was pretty unpleasant up there [a mountain next to Monte Santo, Ridge 604 or something similar]. From time to time, the enemy made us the target for his mines, which, in our position on and in front of open terrain, was the most nerve-racking thing. In the end, the 12th retreated and I was glad to do likewise. As we ran back into the trench, one man from the 12th ran directly into an exploding shell; I stayed for a while longer in B-Line, then we went forward in the (?) Line under Cadet Netetagul. Afterwards, all to Bayonet Command, glad to have the battle (it was the second, and worse than the first) behind us. Didn't know what was going to happen next. Found out only at midnight: retreat.

24 August

At 1.30 am the Company was to break away from the enemy. We [the Company] occupied the old C-Line again and, since the rifles and then the Line(s) in front were ahead of us, we were the last to do so. I hurried along with Jenkner to the Line, but a convoy of the wounded arrived, so I stayed behind with Company Orderly Friedberg and did not manage to get to the Line for a while. I hopped out to see if I could find any remnants of the Line; back to Boroevic Camp [actually forwards]. At 3 o'clock evacuated the camp; bombardment; early morning reached the former site of our battle train [behind the former front], where a Jewish comrade fetched us bread, tinned food and hot coffee. Slept a short time, disturbed by aircraft, climbed a hill at 10am up to the road to Lokve; there put my rifle and rucksack on a cart, then had to keep pace with that. A man from the 6th came towards me; he had been on outpost duty and had been forgotten, so he had made his own way alone out of the 1st Line. My next destination was Foglaria [Voglarji, c. 2 km SW of Lokve], where our Regiment had been for rehabilitation in June/July. Whether we are going into positions again, and where, I should like to know.

29 August

After a long search found Foglaria and slept in a house that Jenkner had requisitioned. The 25th was a bit of a recuperation day, went round and looked up a few acquaintances in the other Companies. In the evening forward and into position, our Company in reserve. We had to occupy the position by day by means of listening posts and by night using a whole platoon, while the rest of the troops stayed back. Position partially chiselled out of stone, partially non-existent. I 'lived' in a cave shelter about 150 [m?] away from the platoon, quite pretty there, but dreadful memory of the three days spent there of lack of water; I became so weak and exhausted that I could scarcely move. When at last I had a proper drink of water, and dirty rainwater at that, yesterday evening, I felt immediately revived; the lack of water will probably persist, however. The quality of the food leaves plenty to be desired, too: tins, bread; day before yesterday no soup because of the shortage of water. Coffee only at 1 am. From now on we draw our rations at nightfall or later. What we eat during the day is then each man's own affair. Yesterday advanced further at the edge of a doline; had to seek really good cover, as it was amazing how often the flyers sought us out. If the Good Lord were to decide to let it rain just now, we should be in a fine state.

On the 24th our Regiment [No. 41 – Czernowitz] [Chernivtsi, western Ukraine] was mentioned in a bulletin. 'In all the trenches they stood their ground.' … true, of course, but since everybody had stood their ground, we went ahead and beat a retreat. In the bulletin of 4 August the drumfire on Monte Santo was mentioned: this was what we had had to put up with when we were advancing to our position. In the *Wiener Journal* it says, among other things, 'our warmest thanks are due to every soldier who holds out in the course of these frightful battles'. Yes, indeed, 'holding out' is the name of the game in this type of combat.

30 August

Yesterday evening there was an alarm, only nothing special happened. I think pickets [outposts] were firing at each other with rifles and this developed into a fine shooting match. We retaliated with artillery fire, probably too short-lived, though, because of the rain! Consequently there were strikes in our immediate vicinity, fortunately no hits. It is more unpleasant to be shot at by our own artillery than by the enemy's; one feels so helpless in the face of our own men. Our artillery was silenced by the firing of flare cartridges. Added to this was the rain, which reduced us to downright despair. It makes one want to tear one's clothes and weep. And it was so cold at night too! My clothes stuck to my body. Wrapped up in a wet blanket and lying on a wet coat, I slept [nonetheless] on and off until early morning, waking up even wetter than during the night. When the much longed-for sun rose, it permitted us to dry out but also brought the return of unbearable thirst, which turned the pleasant weather into a form of torment. Relief is supposed to occur in a day or two.

31 August

Yesterday our friend Seidl ran straight into the arms of the Italians; however, under rifle fire from the Italians on outpost duty, he took to his heels, having most probably shot a man. One man from his patrol wounded; I had the patrol after him; it was announced that there would be a firing trap set by the fighting patrol at 11am, which might easily call forth an Italian attack. Promotion yesterday (some people were passed over), in my case to Patrol Leader.

2 September

Yesterday we ranks moved into the front line and received orders there to use the whole Company to occupy the front line; the 12th Company shifted over to the left. Positions not yet properly dug, in places not even knee-deep; but we made short work of them – not many stones. On duty yesterday; a fairly serious business, as surprise attacks came irregularly – dense, impenetrable forest in front of us. Pestered by aircraft. Was just sitting on a rock a few paces in front of the position when several bombs fell around me close by; thought I'd 'copped it' this time, but was unharmed. By contrast, the man at the listening post in front of us came running back with a head wound. Having waited until the danger from aircraft had slackened off, relieved the listening posts, to find there was a man missing on the left flank; thought he had gone into hiding, hoped he would return to the trench; in the evening he was found dead in some bushes. Pocketed a colossal amount of 'finery' belonging to the lieutenant and even Jenkner opened his mouth with the clear intention of reprimanding me [but thought better of it]. I had picked out his sentry, whose name was Kuza [he was the first who had to mount guard for the second time] and, before I had taken him with me [to go on duty, in this case outpost duty], he had wanted to cut himself an extra slice of bread and put it in his pocket; I refused him permission [according to the regulations, nothing was allowed to interfere with the observer's concentration … this was apparently my reasoning at the time], with the comment that there would be time enough for that after he was relieved. And now he had been 'relieved' without eating the bread. New duty arrangements. Every man is on duty 2 x 3 hours. At night: one commanding officer and four men on sentry duty. Our opposite numbers kept up a high level of activity last night; little opportunity or inclination for sleeping. Cloudy today, which has three advantages: flyers leave us alone, ditto flies, and also it is not too hot. Yesterday at last supplied with 'water' again … brown liquid, afterwards regretted having filled up my canteen with it; coffee considerably more refreshing. An additional nuisance: sleeplessness, at night too. Otherwise well and so ravenous I can hardly make do with the bread I get [still relatively good, worse later], but hankering for variety in the food [soup with potatoes or similar according to circumstances, occasionally with meat too; half a loaf of bread; water].

8 September

In reserve again (Brigade reserve). On outpost duty during the night Monday–Tuesday. There is no outpost position. Shelling with grenades at 4am (mines cannot reach us here, thank goodness). As I awoke and stood up there was a dead man about 25 paces in front of me; also several wounded at the time.

Aircraft. In the night 6th/7th I had to supervise the work detail – a few grenades fell near me. I was at a spot just in between two cave shelter openings and slipped into one of these slit openings at what seemed the proper moment. Hardly in when a grenade hit a spot not more than 10 paces away from where I had been sitting.

We are now being given white bread, not very nutritious, and are all hungry, I in particular more than ever before. Lice multiplying alarmingly and still no certainty of rehabilitation soon. 29th and 30th Marching Battalions have attached themselves to us, including a

Company from I. R. 95. Today we were joined by Tyrolean Imperial Rifles; of their entire number only a few are actually from Tyrol, most are Upper Silesian Poles.

10 September

Yesterday evening relief, which entailed plenty of marching. The 2nd Bayonets (whom we are relieving) constitute the left flank of the Brigade. Nevertheless, positions have been partly dug.

Yesterday I lined up in the Regimental HQ Command among those who had been awarded the small silver medal for bravery. I was recommended for 'the big one'. The medals for bravery on the Italian front are actually more like medals for 'endurance'.

15 September

Crawling with lice; rain since the 13th [spent the whole night standing in the rain]. These lice cause so much misery that one is reluctant to do anything at all. Thorough 'cleansing' yesterday; swarming all over again today. As soon as we get back to the Regimental Reserve I shall go to the sick bay. What is really infuriating is all the talk about rehabilitation and in the end only the 4th Bayonets come and we end up in the tatty old Regimental Reserve, which is only marginally better than the position. Even my imminent promotion to Candidate Cadet [equivalent to Sergeant] and the improved conditions associated with it [officers' mess and probably a batman] can't do anything to make my outlook seem any rosier. Rain since the 13th very heavy during the night, persisted the whole of the next day. Took over my first platoon on the 13th, consequently I have a shelter (only a hole in the wall), which would protect me from the rain; only it is not raining any more and so all I get from my shelter is the lice among the leaves concentrated into a small space. Lack of matches is calamity plain and simple. Not enough cigarette paper available either.

Evidence of the indifference and laziness of the gentlemen further back. Lots of people smoke the pipe tobacco rolled in the paper that contains the tobacco.

Water frightfully dirty; something else that could be avoided.

Flies in unbelievable numbers; the dirt, etc., attracts them.

28 September

13 days (since last entry) of the 'Time spent in service, which is time that stands still'. While on duty I had to put up with a lot from Lt. Denenfeld; sometimes justified, for I was really rather lazy; apparently anti-Semitism too? 23.8 [?] in position again; I was there by the 22nd, to set up my 'quarters'.

Wretched position, hardly anything in the way of 'accommodation', desolate when it rains. 'Not for me', and now I have a firm resolve, strengthened by Denenfeld's unfriendliness, to withdraw from all this somewhat. Evening of 24th went to the sick bay, having had diarrhoea for a while [beforehand, being ill and lacking appetite, had exchanged about 1 ¼ times my bread ration for a pair of underpants]. As I expected, I was ordered there to go to the Regimental infirmary.

Troop transport on the Asiago plateau. Photo courtesy of libreria_il_tempo_che_fu

Wandered along with the pack animals as far as the [Regimental] train; got there 3 am. Hung around there until after the midday meal, 4pm, went up onto the Lokve-Predmeja road [Lokve c. 20 km east of Rijeka; Predmeja c. 30 km north of Rijeka]. The infirmary was supposed to be near Predmeja. By waggon and cart to Predmeja; not a living soul knew a thing about any infirmary.

So – heigh-ho! – off to Haidenschaft [now Ajdovščina, c. 5 km NE of Lokve]. Arrived there in the evening, reported to the field, hospital, was bathed there (shower-bath), deloused and stuck in a decent bed ... three priceless pleasures. On 26th transferred to a section for suspected cases of dysentery. Still here, but it could happen that we will have to go back some way, as everything here is full up.

I am almost well again anyway; the consequence for me, if we withdraw to a hospital farther from the front, could be that I might be given recuperation leave in Vienna. The Regiment does not of course know where I am, whether on the return journey I may encounter difficulties? [None.] I'm not getting on well with the invalid food: hardly anything but liquids and even then only a small spoonful of each. Of course I have bread – a forbidden item in my diet – in my rucksack, to fill out the rations and to ensure that I am not fully recovered too quickly. I have cigarettes too.

5 October

Day of joy and happiness. The sun is shining brightly, but it is even sunnier in my heart. Is it true? Is my wish to come true? I'm going to Vienna! Evening of 29th left Haidenschaft in livestock waggon, in which room had to be found for 33 patients with infections, bound for Laibach [Ljubljana], arrived 2.30pm. Apart from tea with rusk early in the morning, nothing to eat all day long. Evening soup and a dish of noodles. Rooms had to be prepared for us first. The hospital is run with typical military mouldiness, a self-contradictory nonsense in many ways. Food ... too little, as long since recovered, but have to remain on diet in hospital. The best news of all: the visiting head physician finds me emaciated and is sending me to a hospital in the interior of the country, not, mercifully, to the convalescent section or, worse, to the collecting point in Laibach [from whence back to the front]. [I was lucky enough to be free of infection by this time, while the other patients had to stay on, possibly to return to the front again when they were better.] In the hospital in Laibach I often climbed over the railings and went into town; on the 3rd I had [what appeared to be] a fairly substantial dinner and then visited a cinema. [The purpose of the shorter escapades was to buy supplies – other foods were scarcely to be had – with the twofold aim of satisfying hunger and of providing a welcome opportunity for those patients who were still sick to prolong their illness by indulging, secretly, of course, in something so blatantly contrary to the diet.] [To my surprise someone came along straight away looking for the 'platoon leader who is to leave with the transport'. This was unexpected because it came so soon and was so unceremonious.] Train went to Teschen [Český Těšín, Czech Republic, about 25 km ESE of Ostrava]; asked the commanding officer, the head physician, whether Vienna might be possible for me [the train went via Vienna] and he half agreed; on my board it already says W [Wien/Vienna].

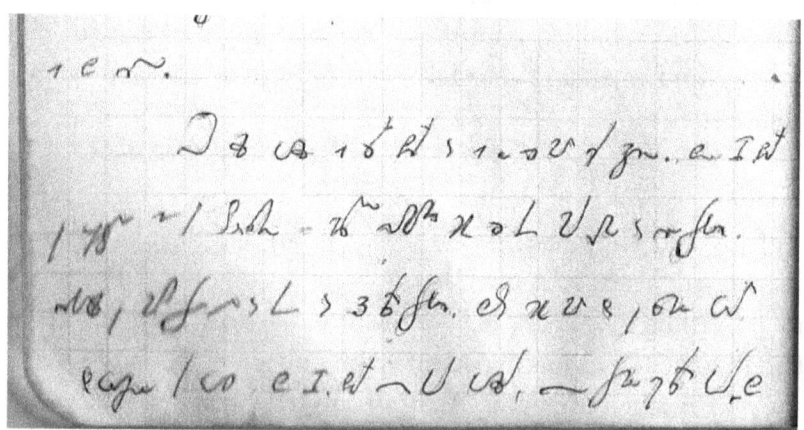

A section of the diary in which Severin describes his diet, food rations and tricks to get more food (text below)

I still get the first food allowance and find it quite appetising. The first allowance for officers is not to be sneezed at. Yesterday afternoon there was tea with rum and a small rusk. The thoughtful warden, who probably doesn't know that the first allowance group don't get any bread, supplemented this with a fairly large piece of bread, which I spread with the cheese that was available. Today, for 10am breakfast [sic; = mid-morning snack], which was two pairs of small oatmeal sausages out of my own pocket ... plus a piece of raisin bread that our divisional warden spread with butter. Breakfast for the other gentlemen was bread and butter, cheese and sausage. And tea for everybody. I'm already curious about the midday meal. It certainly won't fill me up, just like yesterday's dinner, which did not satisfy my hunger, as I'd had to make do all day with the rank and file diet, which consists of soup and a noodle dish and is inadequate. Last night I couldn't sleep for hunger and went and got a few of the leftover small rusks from the serving board.

14 October

11am in Vienna. [Exactly two years to the day later I arrived in Vienna from prisoner-of-war camp.] [The diary closes with these memories of the war from 1917. I reported to the military hospital in Grinzing with a view to asking for admittance, since, having alighted from the train, I should no longer have been able to board it again. The lieutenant who interviewed me told me: 'You are the 13th now who has missed the train', but he let me stay.] A course of arsenic is supposed to help remedy my anaemia. It has the effect of allowing me an extended stay in hospital – which for me is the main thing.

DIARY 1 ENDS HERE

DIARY 2

Editor's note:
This diary was transcribed in 2019–2021, a little more than a hundred years since it was written. It was written in pencil in a small notebook, and the writing has faded over the years. Moreover, in a document of that age there are occasional blemishes, and it is difficult to tell whether a small mark on a page is part of a shorthand letter or symbol or merely an imperfection in the paper. Hence, there are numerous gaps in the transcription, some of which are indicated by square brackets; a few others, where the context showed that they would have been words or phrases of minor importance, have simply been omitted.

Val Frenzela, scene of fighting described in Diary 2. Photo courtesy of libreria_il_tempo_che_fu

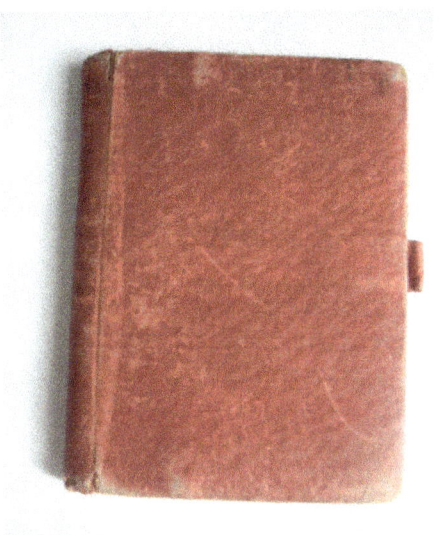

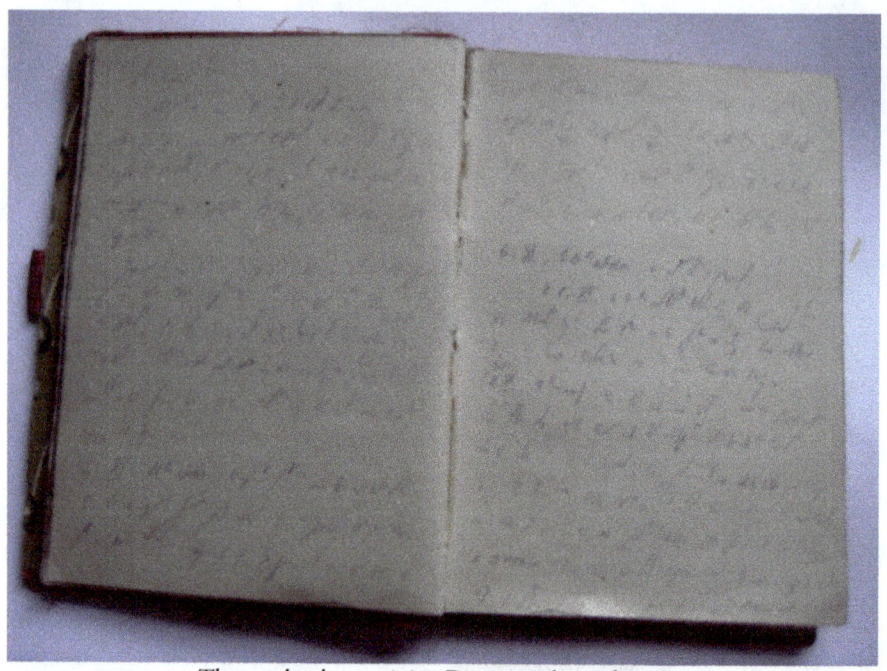
The notebook containing Diary 2 and sample pages

THE DIARY
Covers September 1918 to September/October 1919

ITINERARY

[Modern names given here, insofar as they are known]

1918
15.9   Departure from Merano, Bolzano
15 and 16.9 Trento
17.9   Arrival in Malé
18.9   Report to the Regiment
19.9   Mezzolombardo
20.9 04:00   Arrival in Brenta
22.9 am   Entry into Pieve Tesino

26.9	March from Pieve Tesino towards Grigno
27.9	Leaving the Regimental train
28.9	Towards Barricata
29.9	To Fontana Trepale
2.10	Interview/presentation for Corps certificate
4.10	III and II [?]Bayonets in position
8.10	Reprimand from [?]
19.10	I [?]Bayonets in position, II in camp
22.10	Departure for Val Frenzela
31.10	Retreat (Fontana Trepale, supply train)
1-12.11	On Monte Chiesa
2.11	Chiesa – Sterzinger camp before Monte Rover
3.11	Monte Rover, Caldonazzo, Pergine, Trento Taken prisoner
4.11	Ceasefire
5.11	To Rovereto
6.11	To Ala
9.11	To Avio
11-12.11	To Mozzecane
10.12	To Castel San Pietro, Verona
15-18.12	En route
18.12	Arrival in Mola di Bari

1919

15.1	P. V. Bl. No. 6 ([?] supplement to the liquidated War Ministry), designated Lt. in the Res[erve] [2233], on 1.8.1918, from 1.9.1918

10.10	Departure
12.10	In Villach
14.10	Vienna
evening	

1918

What am I actually keeping a diary for! Surely not because the events that will be recorded here are worth being recorded? – better they should be forgotten. But a memory of these things can prove to be good one day – a small check on someone who is always dissatisfied – if one believes one has really experienced this and hasn't yet consciously lived it.

Anyway, I'm writing in the first instance for me and for now, all with a view to keeping the experiences fresh in my memory, and only secondarily for other people.

In quite similar circumstances to the end of June, I met the Regiment. On the 18th, in the afternoon, I arrived in Malé and learnt that the Regimental HQ would soon arrive in Malé too. The 18th Infantry Division will be sent back to the earlier front section. I was provisionally assigned to the technical company. My company commander comes from Leopoldstadt [a district of Vienna], goes by the name of Kriesch, a coarse-tempered German, whom one has to treat well and yet under whose command one should get on all right. The cadet Schmeisser is not very likeable. The One-year Volunteer Rebensaft is half Viennese.

My wish is thus granted to be with someone with whom I can talk about the things that matter to me most. Much to my joy, my batman is a machine fitter from Simmering.

We spent the 18th in Malé. In the night we were finally dispatched and arrived in Mezzolombardo. No quarters had been arranged for me, so I attached myself to a lieutenant and a second lieutenant, who were also on the hunt for quarters. After some useless efforts and it had become obvious that we were hopelessly stranded, the billeting officer probably wanted to get us off his back and led us to a house, which he called a home for girls. Only on the next day, when the lieutenant and the second lieutenant had long since gone, did I learn from the base commander himself, in not very polite terms, that this house really was a home for girls, namely a barracks for female assistants. What a thing!

In the evening we marched towards San Michele [San Michele all'Adige]. At night we set off and yesterday at 4pm we arrived here in Brenz, I with a raging hunger, as I had carelessly left my batman with my baggage behind at the mobile mess in Mezzolombardo and the transport from there was delayed. It still hasn't arrived.

To my great dismay, I can't post any mail. If I could at least write more … but my writing paper is in the rucksack that I left behind.

Kriesch tried to entertain us, and this is usually good value. Yesterday, in San Michele, Kriesch improvised a story. A Jew has the intention to desert by going backwards. He runs on and on, then all of a sudden he runs into someone who barks, 'Who goes there!' Now the Jew recognises that this is the army chaplain, and calls out, 'God in heaven, have I really got so far going backwards?' To which our Klasinz said, 'Yes, but he didn't manage the technical part.'

28 September [1918]

On the 22nd at 7 o'clock in the morning went by truck, which had also organised the transport of our baggage, to Pieve Tesino. It was a good journey, made at top speed, so I had to give up the idea of taking a book out of my pocket and reading, as I'd intended to do. After two hours, arrived in Pieve Tesino and I reported to my relatively comfortable quarters in one of the tallest houses on the side of a hill slope. Unfortunately, the feeling of comfort didn't last long, as fever with intestinal catarrh, as well as the unexpectedly rapid march, made it impossible for me to settle in as I would have wished, to catch up with the writing I'd missed and to read my books. So, on the 26th, around midday, I had to go with the company down to Grigno, in spite of having had a fever not long before of 38.6°C (the thermometer may not be accurate). Over dinner we joined up with the Regimental HQ in the mess at Grigno. Where were we headed? That was the question on everyone's mind. So off we went to the 1ˢᵗ Army, a section of the 11ᵗʰ Army, and then to the place where the Regiment had set itself up in June. Just a quick bite at table, as everyone prepared for departure, was enough to bury all our hopes for a better option. OK, so be it. [Testwir] is still good fun in the mess. The next day, I had to busy myself as consignment officer for the [new incumbent in charge of the] Regiment in Tollo. It wasn't until 1 o'clock at night that I finally finished loading the materiel and baggage on to the cable railway, and, after a short, deep sleep, I set off with my own people. We had little rest. If you can manage to overlook all the little crosses representing war, it is actually a breathtakingly beautiful area.

K.u.K. Infantry Regiment "Erzherzog Eugen" No. 41
Founded: 1701 – XI. Army corps – 30. Infantry troop division
Ethnic composition: 27 % Ruthenians [East Slavs] – 54 % Romanians – 15 % Poles – 4 % other
Regimental languages: Polish, Romanian
Recruiting district command, Replacement battalion cadre: Czernowitz [Chernivtsi]
Garrison: Czernowitz [Chernivtsi]
Commander: Colonel Eberhard Mayerhoffer von Vedropolje
Staff officers:
First lieutenants: Artur Neumann, Gustav Hartmann, Karl v. Rottenberger, Johann Maxymowicz
Majors: Richard Dworžak v. Kulmburg, Alexander Lapčevič, Johann Hellering
German uniform – Background colour: sulphur yellow – Buttons: white

29 September 4pm

After a strenuous detour via Abasti, we arrived in Barricata just before 1pm. It makes a relatively good impression. The plan for the train group commandos was completely unpredictable. As I neither could nor wanted to undertake a second march for a few days, I travelled via a small cable railway to Marcesina. That was a fun ride. From there, with our troops to Infantry Regiment 142, in a camp. In Barricata I had met Lt. Risson, who triggered for me many memories of Lemberg [Lviv].

Nobody from supplies had arrived at the camp by evening, so I set off on a search for a section of the regiment, hoping to find the Company, if possible, but it soon became too dark. I turned back, to find Robust standing on the road, utterly alone. So, where are the companies, why aren't they here, where is the adjutant? He then delivered a speech about the destinations and goals of the battalion. When I remarked that I had not seen the companies designated on the marching plan marching along the route, he went on disputing the point with me. Where had I been, there or there, had I seen the old Italian positions where the companies had gone? Indeed, I had not seen the Italian positions, and that was just grist to his mill. If you arrive somewhere, you have to look around! Well, for one thing, the Italian positions are not of themselves interesting enough for me to pay any close attention to them, and, for another, I have resolved to experience as little as possible here, to do my duty in the most perfunctory way and to distance myself from it as far as possible in all my thoughts.

I made myself comfortable in an abandoned but cool, well-appointed barracks, had a very long sleep, though with interruptions, as it was rather cold in the night; we were after all at an altitude of more than 1,500 metres. The next day, the technical company was split up into battalions. I was assigned to a platoon in the 3rd Battalion (which I had chosen in preference to the 2nd, that is, in preference to being under the heel of Strobel).

As a matter of fact, the present posting is a bit of a waste for someone who appreciates nature and beauty.

Officers' quarters crowded, men out in the open. Expected stay here 2–3 days.

8 October 5pm

On the 4th, Battalions III and II went to take up their positions. Battalion I and 12 companies remain in reserve. I have the job, with a technical platoon (in reality only 15 men) of fixing up the D-camp. A lot of work, lots of running around, lots of messages coming in from our side. In all, little of interest. An hour ago, a wounded man from the 3rd company turned up right behind our barracks. I get hardly any news from my loved ones and so it was hard for me to motivate myself in light of the monotony that we have to put up with, but which is hard to do, and try to see some better outcomes from work that has accomplished nothing.

10 October 4.30pm

Things are beginning to kick off here, if only a bit. The Italians have been firing almost continuously into the valley that lies to our north, especially into F-camp. The explosions that have followed, being pretty close by, shattered all the glassware and woodwork. Otherwise, the situation is not very dangerous; just once I escaped an accident when a small stone flew right by me. Today is a sad day. The news of the death of senior doctor Fr. put us all in a subdued mood. Along with a first-aider, he had been hit on the head by a [shell] that had broken through the roof of the barracks. Both died on the spot. Fr. was a highly educated man, a friendly German, one of those people who bravely adapt to any circumstances and a person whom one would have wished to survive to the end of the war in good health.

Also, just keeping up the hope that there will be a ceasefire soon works wonders. And nobody cares how peace will be concluded and when that will be, if only this war would come to an end.

11 October 8.30am

What an evil night we have had. The rain was unpleasant in two ways. For one thing, the leaking felt roof let the water through; and for another, the enemy firing into F-camp fell too short. And when you are being kept awake like this, you start to think something that, in the light of day, appears highly unlikely, namely that our barracks could be hit, but which at night seems quite possible. Also, you can see the consequences of such an event much more clearly.

The officers are all at their camp, catching up on missed sleep. The Italian battery is wrapped in silence.

Val Frenzela in winter. Source: Google Maps

Just now my batman has pointed out to me that an unexploded grenade is lying a few steps in front of our window: it is a 15-cm grenade, of probably French origin. The Italians will doubtless have enough bombs. Our artillery had replied very comprehensively.

12 October 3.30pm

Cadet Herzeiser from the technical company has fallen, how I don't yet know. He had only been in action for two days. Moreover, there have apparently been many gas poisoning victims.

Last night various exciting stories kept us awake until 1am. First there was talk about how our night-time warfare is going. Then we moved on to other things. As we did not come to any agreement, we ended up talking about how these conversations are conducted and what we hoped to get out of them. My advantage in the majority of these discussions is that I'm the youngest.

12 October 6 o'clock
Last night's enemy fire preceded an attack on a section of the positions of our division. 5th/117th Company was repulsed and a machine-gun was requested. Lt. Stumm, likewise of the […] company, is the star of the day. Five prisoners were taken from the Italians. The Italian officer knows nothing about the ceasefire. Stumm sustained some light wounds and has been evacuated.

22 October 12.30pm
This morning I received the order to depart with my platoon and head towards the Frenzela zone. I'm OK with that, as it's possible I will like it better than here.

23/24 October 00.30am
The march towards the Frenzela gorge went off fairly uneventfully, that is to say, I didn't even walk much. Aside from ignorance of the route, that would have been really difficult. The officers and their staff and so on have been put up in relative comfort in barracks. Even the men of the regimental headquarters have a roof over their heads. This evening Lt. Kratschek and Warrant Officer Weltschar and I were on duty. There were changes of position … and every time we learnt a bit more. At the time, when I was up there, you could hardly hear a single shot. The colonel was with the [?] command, something to do with an attack expected today. In the event of a breakthrough, the technical company should join up with the 10th and head for a ridge north of the Frenzela positions, which will surely be the target of the heaviest artillery fire. I have a feeling that nothing will come of this, nothing of the attack, not to mention the tactical use of the technical units, which Lt. Kriesch

withdrew from last time. Artillery fire from our side started up about half an hour ago.

24 October 4.30am
The artillery fire started by orders given through or perhaps in response to the expected attack did not last long. However, since then, the Italians have replied with greater intensity. In the western part of the Frenzela positions it was quite bad. For a while, we all squeezed into the cave shelter until, after three hours, things died down a bit and we realised that the big attack was not going to happen, so we all came out, one by one. My batman has got a fragment of an explosive device in his lower leg. Apparently it's nothing dangerous. Strangely enough, when I returned in the evening and expressed my dissatisfaction with him over some minor thing, I said to him: 'Today is your last day with me, tomorrow you'll have someone else!' And that actually happened, although in a way differently from what Still had imagined.

The firing goes on, but [...] couldn't stop me from going to bed in spite of it.

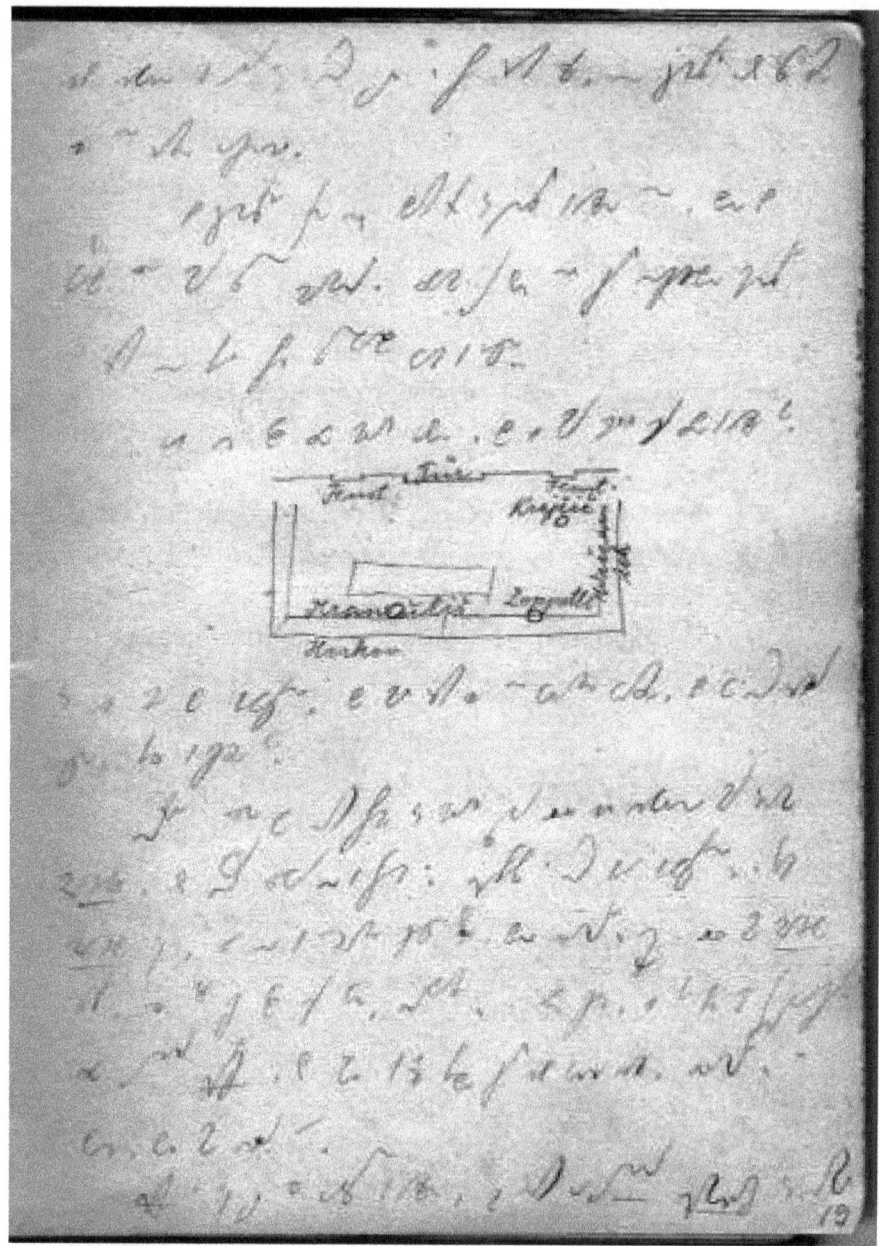

The diary page of this section, with floor plan of Severin's room showing the names of his roommates, as well as the location of the door and two windows

27 October 1pm

It's very calm and muddy again in the Frenzela gorge, as though nothing had happened, absolutely nothing.

Yesterday evening was fairly comfortable. We slept, with interruptions as usual, till nearly 8am. Warrant Officer Werfer, who rolled up with his platoon at 3 o'clock, insisted he was utterly convinced that something would still happen today.

As we all woke up around the same time – probably because of an explosion nearby – the Italian artillery was already in action. So we got dressed. Lt. Zoppetti was ready first. We who slept on the upper bunks considered getting up for a bit, but when there were two strikes nearby we got dressed in a hurry. I was just debating whether I should have a wash or not, when, as we confirmed later, an approximately 15-cm grenade fell 17 paces from our barracks.

The right side of Lt. Zoppetti's scalp and part of his brain were torn off, his eye hung down from its socket. He died on the spot. Krejčić (cadet trainee) suffered an arm wound, and his guts were hanging out; bandaging was out of the question; apparently he died two hours later. Warrant Officer Werfer was struck in the chest with some fragments of explosive. Two batmen were slightly hurt. From the same grenade, Rebensaft, who a few seconds earlier had run towards the cave shelter, was hit in the thigh before he got there by a piece of explosive or a small stone.

These bits of the explosive device can only have entered through the door and window, as the wounds were covered with stones. The blast from an explosive device that hit later tore part of the stone wall away.

I can still count myself lucky to have escaped unhurt.

And I have the sense that, in the next few weeks that we will have to hold out, nothing will happen.

Naturally, after this misfortune, we had to go immediately to the cave shelter with our Herkov, who even now wasn't fully dressed. Krejčić was still conscious. He asked Herkov to send greetings to his family, then requested coffee. When Herkov told him it would be all right, he replied nervously, 'but I'm completely mangled'. He asked for a blanket from Lt. Kriesch, who came into the cave shelter an hour and a half later, as he was cold.

Kriesch had come on the colonel's order to check on First Lt. Kramačlić and me. Kramačlić was as good as dead in the next shelter. As the fierce shellings became fewer and further between, we returned to the barracks. Rebensaft was still in a good enough state to be able to thank his lucky stars for his escape. He left, much envied by all.

In the afternoon it was generally quiet, in the evening and all night long there was occasional heavy artillery fire into the battlefield or, rather, into the hillside opposite. As we didn't want to expose ourselves to danger unnecessarily, we retreated to the cave shelter every time – three or four times during the night – which meant we hardly had a chance to get to sleep, not until the morning, since when it has been completely quiet.

Yesterday the companies did not receive any support; people were left properly hungry with only their tinned food. Naturally no post arrived, nor did any go out.

The Italian artillery fire was of course only subsidiary to the actions on the Col del Rosso. There were three groups of people: prisoners, wounded and plenty of dead. Every day there are deserters from the company. Lt. Fren, Trainee Cadet Tromaschetz, Sergeant Sawedlaus have gone over to the enemy, also Scharschen from the 12th Company. Although no one has expressed out loud the view that anyone can defect if he thinks it is to his advantage, we hope the defectors will keep their mouths shut. It is possible that the direct hits on the Frenzela gorge were attributable to information given by Sawedlaus.

The company has suffered so many losses of men, and of officers as well. Every day one or two officers are sent off to the hospital, which naturally delights us no end. The company numbers 40–70 men. In mid-December, not a single company had fewer than 200 men. We can't go on in this vicious circle much longer.

The state of the people, positions and cave shelters and the conditions defy all description.

A telegram that just arrived says that 16 men of the supply group were killed by gas bombs; 10 horses also died.

We assume that those people who go on leave will not come back again.

Tension is growing with our reluctance to expose ourselves to Italian shells and mines any longer.

Until now I have been able to keep myself free of lice; today I may already have some of these guests, although I haven't yet checked.

[I doubt] whether any of us cares what will happen to Austria and the other nations!

29 October 7pm

Today it was fairly quiet; yesterday was also a reasonable day. To be sure, the Italians have still been in action every night. In the 3rd, 1st and 12th Company there was one man dead, as well as several wounded. Probably victims of our prematurely and hastily mounted barrage.

This afternoon Duberg, from our company, was wounded.

Kriesch, Kratschek and I retreated to the cave shelter. And we slept surprisingly well there, having had couches placed under the bedding. There were drips coming from the 'stalactites' that had formed on the concrete ceiling. This was quite a minor inconvenience, compared with the advantages.

31 October 4am
I returned to the front line an hour ago, to find the barracks empty, most of the regimental headquarters having marched off, including the technical company. I have to follow.

Today my people worked first of all in the trenches, then on the wire barriers at the outpost of the 12th Company. Suddenly there was an attack on the 2nd outpost of the 1st Company.

1 November 9am
Suddenly [there was firing towards] the hillside opposite and into the gorge, which forced us to retreat to the cave shelter.

When the attack happened, I withdrew with my men, waited for the end of the action and then went down through the prickly shrubs into the Frenzela gorge. My heelless and soleless shoes were real works of art, like those you might expect to see on a wire-walker who can mostly avoid falling off the wire. However, at least I pulled off a few clever little tricks … of the kind my dear mother is acquainted with, insofar as we can mention these kinds of tales at all. At 3 o'clock I arrived down below and learnt about the march that had happened. As it had become quieter, we headed off at 6 o'clock, in a small group of seven men, through the Merla gorge to Fontana Trepale, which we got to, having walked through the night, three hours earlier than planned. It was not particularly pleasant there. A shell that had fallen near the barracks of the technical company had wounded two of our people. Towards evening, we went for supplies.

I'm just glad to be rid of the prickles. Order followed order. Now we know finally that we have to occupy the position and the positions are now about as rundown as before the 12th offensive; they are supposed to be better than the ones we have encountered so far, which one can well believe. This evening we set off on the march.

It's not only during an offensive that one can't work but also during a retreat. [?], tights, trousers, shoes, etc., are my booty from the regimental supplies. But then I had to open my trunk, which I couldn't take with me, and pack the contents in rucksacks; less essential items were left behind. Apart from my batman's, I have to help carry that of another man in the company.

2 October 11pm
Today was particularly eventful. What I went through today seems to have happened some days ago.

The huge exertions have made me so tired that, after eating a questionable meal consisting of requisitioned potatoes and coffee, I'm not, with the best will in the world, in any state to write about today and yesterday in any detail. However, that is exactly what is needed at this point, because I can't know what the next hour will bring.

6 November 5.30pm
Taken prisoner by the Italians.

On 1.11 at 3pm we broke off from the supply of our regiment. Everything went in a fairly orderly fashion, but then came [...] and the march became endless.

7 October [should read 7 November] 9am
Marched with short breaks and a longer, maybe two-hour, rest, including in a camp, which lasted until 2 o'clock.

Even the rest was disturbed, as defective cars were being chucked out off the street. In a division commando's car, you might see the retreat as romantic, but it wasn't so for the infantry. Our goal was Monte Chiesa, over 2,000 metres high, where we were supposed to encamp at that position. The men moved into the position pretty well.

The technical company, as well as the disarmed marching company and M. G. Company, without munitions, [...] stayed behind, in very well organised and well-kept stone-built barracks. We three from the technical unit were allocated a truly delightful room. The door had glass panels. The borders of the walls were even furnished with paintings. And there were two stools and three bedsteads. We installed ourselves straight away, as if it had been decided we would be there for a longer stay. After we had brewed and drunk tea, we went to bed. It was perhaps half past four when we went to sleep. Well provided with blankets and almost fully undressed. An alarm sounded at 7 o'clock. So we quickly dressed. Kriesch had command over the company positioned below. Retreat, destination unknown. Totally drained, we set off. Losing our way, as on the day before, tiredness and [...]. A kind of depot set up. In the end, I couldn't go on carrying my rucksack and loaded it on to a transport vehicle.

Nevertheless, I trudged laboriously on. At 4 o'clock I arrived at the camp, where we assembled. Around 6 o'clock we set off again; the companies seemed to be pretty much complete. However, a halt was soon called. This was because we were the last of the division and the division commando intended to use us as reserves. We spent the night in Sterzemer camp, as reserves. The enemy seems quite near. Gun and machinegun fire rarely let up.

Requisitioned and cooked potatoes and coffee made a delicious dinner. Naturally I slept the sleep of the dead until trouble in the camp woke us up at 6.30. We got dressed immediately and hurried on our way again in disorderly fashion. On the way, a lieutenant told us that he'd heard some sort of fanfare and therefore believed that a ceasefire had been concluded. A captain from the general staff is supposed to have confirmed this. Anyway, we were going downhill and so we marched on. Towards midday I was in Gallnoetsch [Caldonazzo], where the 117th reassembled and from then on continued together on our trek, destination San Vito.

As I passed Calceranica, an Italian cavalry patrol made an appearance. Lots of running about. It was announced that the meeting place would be south of Bozen [Bolzano].

This meant getting to Trient [Trento] as quickly as possible. Before Pradeschino I got up on to a wagon, whose trek commander was only a platoon leader and who probably enjoyed smoking Kinder [?]. In around six hours I covered 61 km on this wagon. The aircraft base was ablaze. About 7 km from Trient, all this travelling finally became too much for me. I was rested anyway. And so I decided I'd rather ride a few steps and then stay put for a few minutes. To get to Trient *per pedes apostolorum.* It was already nearly night-time (on the 3rd) when I met Link on the way; we wanted to reach Trient quickly so as to be able to visit Ida Ruggera there. What was left of the regiment evidently consisted only of officers. We slipped away (skedaddled) and headed for Trient. Shortly before we reached it we came across the main road again. We had heard about a laying down of weapons in Trient but hadn't given much credence to this rumour; however, the masses of rifles, bayonets, etc., lying on the street set us right. Also on the street stood a harmless patrol consisting of three men.

1941 map of the Bolzano area. Compiled and drawn by the War Office.
Source: Perry-Castenada Map Collection at the University of Texas

Having arrived in Trient, we finally learnt that we were prisoners – everyone, all the many regiments, the whole lot who had marched on the road, the 111th Army and more, all prisoners. As far as the visit to Miss Ruggera went, nothing doing. The rest of the 117th followed us to the campsite. The houses in Trient were decked with green, white and red flags. The population were well pleased with the coming of the Italians, as was to be expected. Civilians armed with revolvers maintained order. Around 3am on the 4th, we were all gathered together and the officers were finally brought, by a roundabout way, to add their number to the fellow-sufferers who had already assembled there. In the morning we were taken to a complex situated outside Trient, where we stayed until 5pm. As there was no sign of Italian food supplies, we commandeered food provisions from a train that was stationed nearby, especially flour. And so it happened that we left Trient by car, completely satiated and in general not unhappy. We continued our cooking of fruits and coffee there. At 6 o'clock we set off again, making a fairly long halt in Rovereto.

An Italian general had a very friendly conversation with an Italian colonel in our midst, Begado, apologised for any inconvenience we might suffer, promised some vehicles, which were unsuitable for marches and which did in fact arrive, and other vehicles for baggage, of which only one turned up. In any case, we wouldn't have made use of this privilege. It would have been too unsafe. After a little rest, we headed off briskly towards Ala. Our colonel passed up the offer of a car to travel in. Wants to stay with his men.

We are now about 3 km north of Ala. After a recce with field glasses, maps and so on, we were put up in very basic houses and each of us received a half portion of jam and a slice of rusk.

Those of us here are all exclusively officers, all from the 117th, with the exception of the second-in-command Linder and Warrant Officer Buseck, who are faithfully sticking with us. Here we met Lt. Diebeck, who had 30,000 K with him, which the colonel divided among us, giving each a share of 1,000 K.

Bank note issued by the Austro-Hungarian Bank. Courtesy Michael Brett private collection

Although we were very tired, we slept very badly. The camp was hard and cold and the wind roared ...

The mood is not too good today. If only we can get away from here soon.

There's a canteen here, where we can buy wine and, at a high price, Mag[r]onie [possibly noodles]. Good that we have enough money for the time being so as not to have to go without.

What has happened and is happening in the former Austria we are finding out from Italian civilians; yesterday we got more accurate information from a warrant officer who had arrived in Trient from Vienna by the U-train and who had delivered coffee. If we had been in the hinterland, we would all already be civilians.

9 November 12.45 pm
Yesterday our really uncomfortable stay near Ala came to an end. 80 German officers departed, supposedly for Ala and from there on to Adino, south of Ala. Our hopes of being transported by wagon were shot to pieces. On the other hand, the camp we are now in is reasonably

well organised and in a tolerable condition. A major is the camp commander, we are quartered in barracks and are supposed to receive warm food and bread, which we are at this moment longing for. Lice are tormenting me and everyone and for that reason we're all very keen to get away from here quickly. In the afternoon, maps are supposed to be distributed; and so I will soon be going home and write to Elli and be able to lay her anxieties to rest.

Expectations of going home soon are quite lively [although] the waves of excitement are no longer so intense and we talk about the news calmly. We only still get agitated thinking about how allowing ourselves to be taken prisoner had been a foregone conclusion and nobody had told us what the real situation was. The premature dissemination of the news about the ceasefire is being interpreted as deliberate.

This morning there was coffee for us; our colonel loyally joins in everything and queues up for coffee with the pretty Italian cup that he got hold of yesterday. The coffee – incidentally – is better than ours.

12 November 2pm

Yesterday afternoon we suddenly got the order to depart. With hopes, which were not fulfilled, we set off. Everyone piled on to wagons and within about an hour and a half the train set off. The journey was not as pleasant as the [earlier one], but parts of the area were really interesting. We made a longish halt outside Verona. Then we were taken to a station about 8 km from Verona, went by night 3-4 km on foot to a camp, which – as it turned out – was already fully occupied, so, after a long wait, we went back the same way. Back on to the wagons, then about an hour's ride on the train until we arrived here at 3am, i.e. in Mozzekan [Mozzecane], or whatever this awful hole is called. We were put up in a large house that was formerly an institute and slept all squeezed in together on the floors of the rooms and in the corridors. This morning I picked up news of a comprehensive demobilisation, and consequently I now feel a bit better. Our provisions arrived a short while ago, a serving of jam and a half loaf of bread among four men, but this was declined by order of three of our warrant officers. The commander of our station (now, after nine days!) promised us generous rations for the evening, namely warm rice soup and a small piece of bread appropriate to the circumstances. My lunch today consisted of chocolate. I'll try to get hold of some bread later.

First letter home after being taken Prisoner of War [mid-November 1918]

My dear ones!

Every time I write, I am assuming that you have not received my previous letters.

At the end of last month, we embarked on a move back to Trient, where we were expected. We could have saved ourselves all this long exertion; it would have been much simpler just to wait in the right town and location to be taken prisoner. From the evening of the 3rd to the afternoon of the 5th in Trient, 6th Rovereto, 7–11th in Avio near Ala; since yesterday here near Verona. We're all well. There are about 20 officers from the 117th here, all sticking together in comradely fashion. I have enough money (c. 1,000 K).

Above all, I wish to be back home with you soon, my dear ones. Everything else is of no consequence.

Please let Elli and all my other friends know.

Affectionate greetings and kisses from

Your devoted Severin

P.S. Don't reply, as we'll presumably be moving on soon.

---

22 November 11am
The days all pass in the same fashion. I can't say that we are in a bad way here; when we had been here for two days, the provisions improved and the quantity is more than enough. Every day we get a loaf of bread and half a litre of wine, at midday a first-rate beef soup and meat, in the evening plenty of rice. Nevertheless, there is a lot of buying and eating going on. Especially chocolate and figs, treats we've been missing for a long time.

Having washed and changed my clothes, I'm not being troubled by lice as much as earlier and before I did so. More in the mood for learning, even if it's only dabbling in learning. Berghof talks to me about judicial, indeed philosophical matters, Marmork about Judaism and Jewish matters and so on. I am reading the [?] Streminanten and am taking an interest in Italian, for practical purposes, such that I can take part in every discussion and every conversation with the Italian soldiers and am already known to some of them as an interpreter. If I have any wishes for material improvements to my situation, it would be first and foremost more opportunities to keep clean and more comfortable living quarters, tables, seat and a bed. The desire to receive post is not so great any more. And that is good, because then I will get used to leaving off writing and going without letters, which is what I will have to do in future.

We do not know how long we will have to stay here.

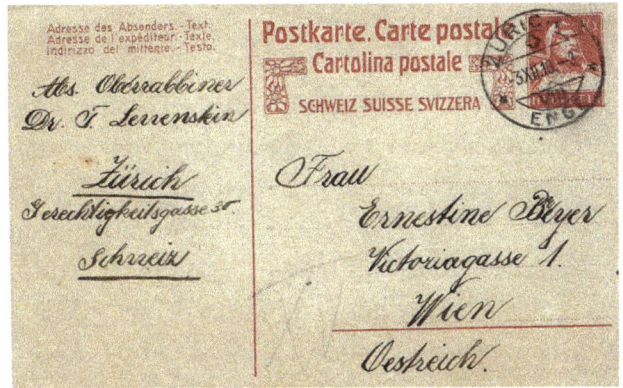

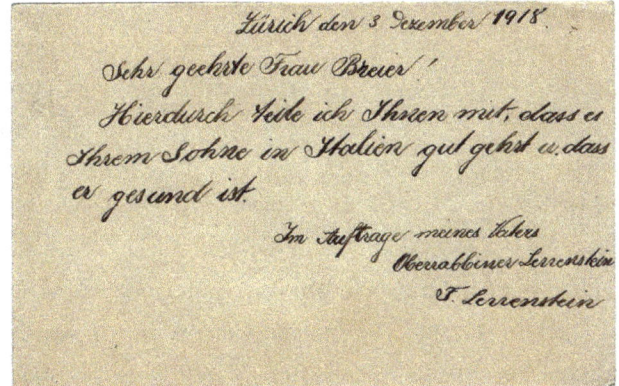

Postcard to Severin's mother

Side 1
Sender: Chief Rabbi Dr. T. Lewenstein, Zurich, Gerechtigkeitsgasse 3, Switzerland
To: Mrs Ernestine Breyer, Victoriagasse 1, Vienna, Austria

Side 2
Zurich, 3 December 1918
Dear Mrs Breier!
I inform you herewith that all is well with your son in Italy and that he is well.
On behalf of my father, Chief Rabbi Lewenstein
T. Lewenstein

---

14 December 4pm

The last few days in Mozzekan turned out to be a bit more pleasant, since we had the chance to go out freely almost every day, and the food became more plentiful. The order to depart came pretty unexpectedly: even to the Italian major who travelled expressly to Verona to get information. What he found out was that our departure was being postponed by a day. Meanwhile, we received our wages, though for what period of time we don't know; we only know that 5 Lire have been deducted to cover our keep, as well as the use of the garden, lavatory and water.

Luckily, we didn't have to carry our rucksacks: we were promised that these would be sent on after us very soon. And in fact on the next evening I was already reunited with my rucksack, from which soap and brush were missing.

On 10 December [entry presumably retrospective]

So, around 11.30am we set off en route via the picturesque Villafranca as far as the gates of Verona. Until then, everything was fine, but then they started (we were already used to this) to make us traipse for three hours outside Verona through all kinds of gates to the fort and back out again. For the first time in many months, I was thoroughly tired by the time we reached our goal, the Castel San Pietro. A gigantic building that suggested mass occupation. How agreeably disabused we were when everything went so smoothly, and we found ourselves installed in rooms, each with a bed with two blankets and two bedsheets. At midday the next day we even got something to eat. The quantity of provisions here is about the same as in Mozzekan, but it should have been better and is supposed to have been cut down only after the cessation of the American push.

Verona lies at our feet – pretty much literally. The view over the city at all times of day is lovely, distinctive and always different.

Our choir will continue rehearsals on Friday; today we put on a 'concert on the terrace': mostly to pass the time for our hungry comrades who were waiting for the delayed lunch.

I'm continuing relatively undiligently to learn Italian. Night-time is the best time: you wrap yourself in blankets and sleep, with a pleasant sensation, on a fairly soft mattress, like at home, maybe even better, and dream of this and that. Mostly we spend the mornings in bed. I would rather get up early now and then. If it weren't rather cold in our room, which is a corridor.

That our blankets and sheets appear to be swarming [with insects] is of no concern to us, we're resigned to it.

Rumour has it that we'll be moving from here soon, towards southern Italy, Lake Como, and so on. The rumours even go so far as to say we're going to America. We have split ourselves into groups of 150 so that those who know one another and want to stay together can go together.

20 December 11am
For the 15th, we had decided to stay in bed one Saturday to recover from the efforts of the work days. Things turn out differently … In the morning we received our wages up to and including the 18th, a significant event. In the afternoon we marched off and, via a shorter route than on the march in, arrived back in the city and at the station.

Actually, we waited around more than we walked. In the evening, we were put on board a train, 30–40 in each saloon-carriage. It was around midnight when we got underway. We were told the destination was Warlatto.

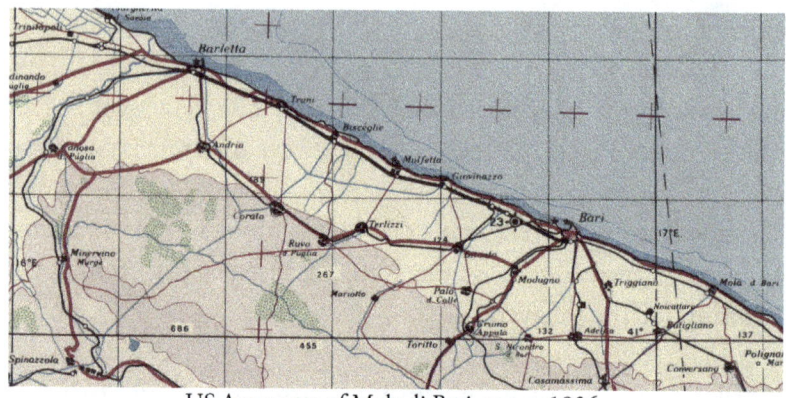

US Army map of Mola di Bari area, c. 1936.
Source: Perry-Castenada Map Collection, University of Texas

After a journey of nearly 60 hours we reached our destination: it is this Mola, south of Bari. The journey passed relatively pleasantly; for hours on end we could look out on the sea. Even the area had a lot to offer that was new. Houses with typical Italian architecture, sea creatures, orange and olive trees, further south cacti, south of Monte Gargano the population is denser, the towns larger and lovelier. Even Mola itself probably has 20–30,000 inhabitants. We got very inadequate provisions ... even at the stations there was little opportunity to buy anything. Besides, the Italians are very dishonest salesmen; they cheat us whenever they possibly can.

In Mola, the former [Grenzaneser] [? Borderlanders] disembarked. Another 85 men were required to stay back. We of the 117th also decided to go with them. The others, about 700 of them, rode on further. The inhabitants of Mola received our huge throng crowding the streets and alleyways in a very friendly fashion.

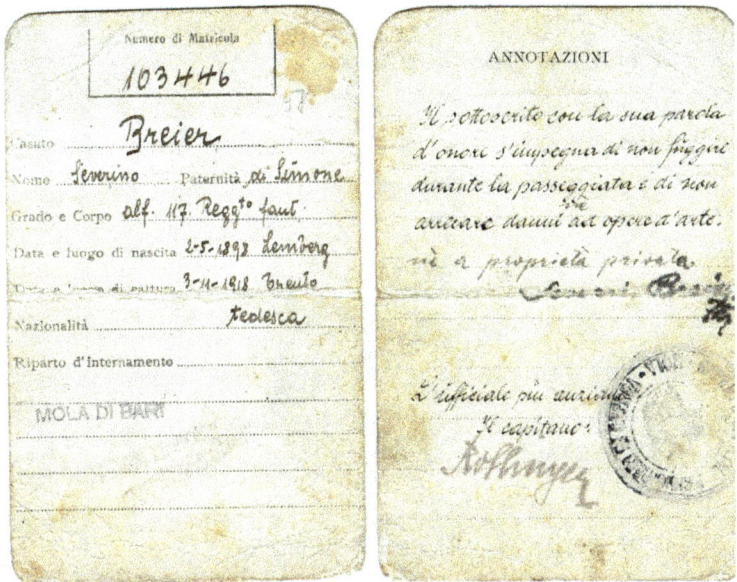

Pledge card

POW pledge card
Side 1
Number on register: 103446
Surname: Breier
Name: Severino
Father's name: Simone
Rank and Regiment: Ensign, 117th Infantry Regiment
Date and place of birth: 2-5-1898 Lemberg
Date and place of capture: 3-11-1918 Trento
Nationality: German
Allocation of internment

Side 2
The undersigned pledges, on his word of honour, not to flee during the journey and not to cause damage to any artwork or private property.

[Signed] Severin Breier

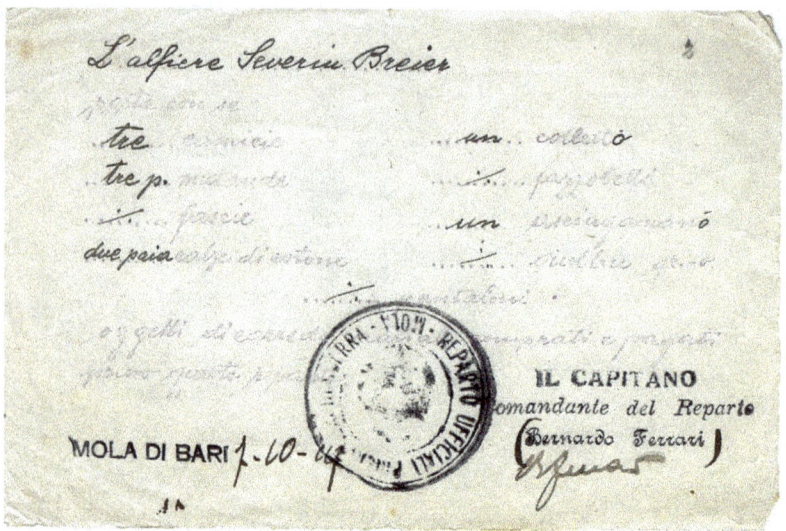

Allocation of clothing

Ensign Severin Breier
Brings with him:
Three shirts
Three pairs of underwear
Two pairs of cotton socks
One collar
One towel
Signed by the Commander of the Department, Mola di Bari

Our camp is not far from the station, almost in the centre of the town. It is a former monastery. There are about 400 of us here. The usual division according to rank was done here for the first time, if not fully. The commandant of the camp, a lieutenant, seems genuinely to be taking the trouble to make our circumstances as pleasant as possible. The officers' mess and canteen will be set up and an officer responsible for domestic arrangements will be appointed from among our midst. Requests will be conveyed to him through the senior officer in charge, an artilleryman. This captain has the authority for this, although he doesn't particularly inspire our confidence. Judging by the way he conducts himself, he could be something like a lieutenant colonel.

The provisions are just about adequate. I don't have the patience to write anything memorable any more, as I have been fully engaged with a Langenscheidt phrasebook belonging to a colleague.

25 December 10am
Even though all our hopes for an improvement in our conditions have not yet been fulfilled, or wholly fulfilled, at least they are a notch above the merely bearable. The officers' mess has been set up. And well equipped. Of course the food, especially the quantity of it, leaves something to be desired. Mostly we get beef, followed by peas and potatoes cooked in oil. The soup is always excellent. Yesterday there was plenty to eat, on the occasion of Christmas Eve.

In fact, yesterday evening passed in high spirits. At 8.30 the courtyard was illuminated with candles, and we sang 'Silent Night' and 'Homewards would I once again'. Fröhlich and Sarninger regaled us with stories, Fröhlich especially had us in fits of laughter the whole time. His interlude with Captain Öllinger, which invited us to be satisfied with the good things, was delightful.

Today about 30 Austrian orderlies arrived, who were fitted out with new uniforms and underwear.

Sarninger and Fröhlich have more or less slept off last night's happenings. Fröhlich had almost caused a disaster yesterday by venting his hatred for Italians against a completely innocent visitor from Lothring [?]: the poor chap was terrified and stood there trembling.

The day before yesterday the second provisions group had the day off. We were taken down to the sea and spent some time nearby. For me, and in fact for most of us, the sea offered us something new and some acquaintance with Italy. The waves slowly rolling in and breaking on the rugged shore. The water flowing into the rivulets and channels, that is the scene ... And the sea in all its powerful grandeur, which offers a glimpse into greatness. As we were going home, the sun was just setting, the sea took on a violet hue and this was reflected in the streets and even on the walls of the houses. And on the sails of boats heading to shore.

Here by the sea it is neither hot nor cold. In the town itself and where we are, by contrast, it's still getting pretty warm. Washing bare-chested in the morning is so pleasant that one does it at one's leisure in the courtyard.

The canteen has quite a lot to offer. Yesterday especially we did a fair bit of shopping. Figs are comparatively cheap and plentiful.

The days pass pretty quickly here. Only you have to make sure you have a supply of candles, so that you're not inclined to doze off when it gets dark. Although I'm not learning much other than Italian, I can't claim to be making rapid strides forward. There are a lot of prerequisites for learning that are missing. Concentration, quiet and so on.

We can send letters off in the post eight times a week, either letters or postcards; naturally, it is nearly always letters that are written.

27 December 6pm

There's a kind of dreary monotony in the days. However, I have promised myself that I'll get a lot out of the courses that our Lt. Fritz has instigated. We're all a bit short of mental activity and this distraction could be a very welcome way of reviving our spirits. On the other hand, following the courses will not take a great deal of effort. There are few materials here ... Today some of the men received iron bed frames with mattresses; probably the rest will get them tomorrow. The courses that have been announced so far are: English for Advanced Students (Lt. Müller), French (Lt. Wiener), English for Beginners

(Müller), Roman Law (Dr. Anders), Transport Systems (First Lt. Klein), The Textile Industry (a different First Lt. Klein), Mechanical Engineering (Captain Findeis) … tomorrow Captain Findeis is going to give a lecture on Large-scale City Transport Systems, which will probably attract many listeners anyway.

Sometimes I am really down in the dumps and can't take any pleasure in anything. In our big room it is always so noisy that you can't think or dream in peace. Then there's the problem of not having enough light, as the candles are unfortunately rather expensive. The most enjoyable thing is in the evening, when the others have gone to bed, to sit at a table on the slope outside and to write or study by the light of a candle.

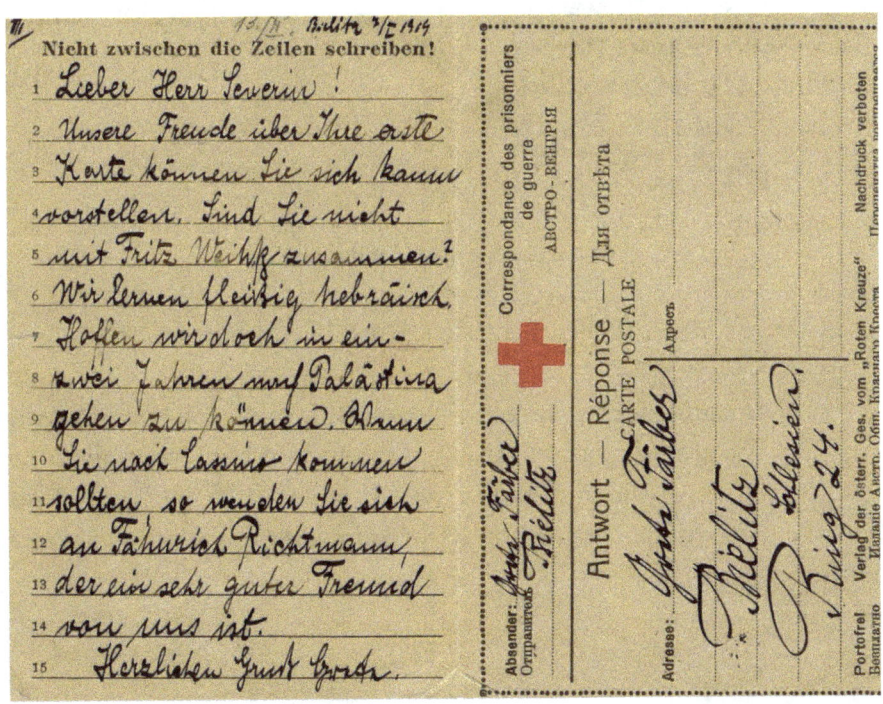

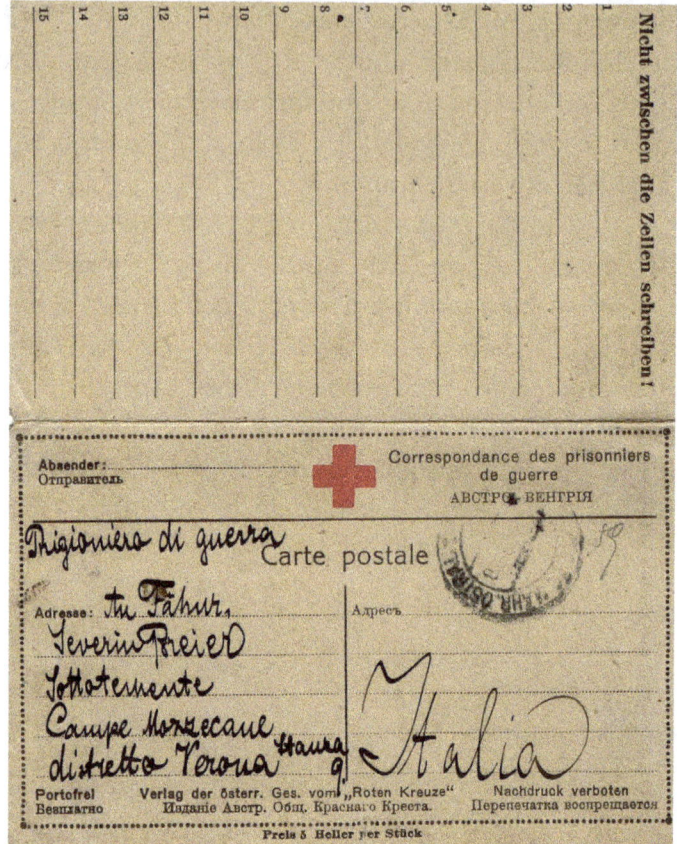

Postcard, delivered by the Red Cross, from Grete Färber, a family friend. Her daughter, Elli, was Severin's girlfriend at the time

From Grete Färber, Bielitz, Schlesien, Ring 24. [3] January 1919
Dear Mr Severin
You can't imagine our joy at receiving your first card. Are you not with Fritz [?]? We are diligently learning Hebrew. We hope after all to be able to go to Palestine in a year or two. If you should find yourself in Cassino, get in touch with Ensign Richtmann, who is a very good friend of ours.
Warmest greetings
Grete

Editor's note:
The following section of Diary 2 is interspersed with extracts from letters and cards sent by Severin to his family. Some are presented in note form.

1919

Prisoners of War in Mola di Bari, 1919.
Front row: Lt. Jungwirth, First Lt. Ledwina, Lt. Fritz, acting Regimental Adjutant, First Lt. Kammler, 1. Reg. Adjutant, ?
Back row: Severin at L, of the other five one is Aufmesser, and the one standing on the far R is Sieringer (or a similar name).
All from 117th Infantry Regiment

26 January 1919 6pm

Still no news from home; but I'm not the only one. A while ago some arguments came up in the mess …. Always the same thing. Electric light, table and benches in the room or bed frames with mattresses and bed linen. Also, plentiful provisions [are needed for our situation]. Anyway … I attended the following courses: Mathematics, English, Roman Law. Other lectures will be given from time to time, which I will of course attend; actually I'm well occupied with Italian. Kohn has provided me with a copy of De Amicis's *Cuore*.

I'm just bored if I'm not studying anything, so I study.

It has got colder. It rains almost every day. The wind is often annoyingly strong.

Now and then we all find that being together all the time gets on our nerves.

26 January 1919
Postcard
From Severin (2nd Lt) in Mola di Bari to Salomon Breier in Vienna
Still no news from you. Please let me know if you have received the 150 K I sent you. It is cool, windy weather here. We are hoping for a return home and a happy reunion soon. Is everyone at home? Have you heard anything from Katowice? From Lemberg? Is everything going on as usual at home? Are you suffering from a shortage of light and coal?

19 February 1918 [should read 1919] 3.30 pm
Today the doctors went off to Eimersee, and tomorrow the Hungarians are leaving for Spilin. There is supposed to be a station at Eimersee. The word is that next week students and teachers will be sent off. I hope this proves to be true, as hope costs nothing and it is actually possible. I am, however, still working pretty hard at my studies, although not as much as I would really like; often I just can't drag myself to it, as I'm too much on edge.

Three days ago, First Lt. Klein, textiles Klein, ran a private course in double-entry bookkeeping, which of course is very welcome to me. On the whole, nothing has happened here that is worth writing about.

Up till now, I have received first a letter and then three cards from home, also three cards from Elli [Färber; his girlfriend], far too few. I was also out in my calculations; naturally, I wanted to go over the maximum of eight letters I'm allowed to write per month, and by the 13th I had already written 12; two further ones the postal officer wanted

...e had already booked the individual items for ... w I have to wait until March.

...sletter will be ready by the middle of the ...scribe to it half-monthly. It often contains really ...eresting items, and there's a fun corner on Sunday.

A few days ago there was a song concert in the inner courtyard, which was definitely artistically of high quality.

5 March 7pm
Yesterday was Fasching Eve. The jollifications were pretty forced; on the other hand, the merriment on Ash Wednesday was genuine. Our mood is getting more and more irritable by the day. As regards trifling things, there are two that come into play. Kraschischobsky [?] is really highly unpleasant; he downright spoils staying in the room for me. Lately I have felt less like studying. Sometimes I'm too much on edge to be able to think straight.

I read articles in the Italian newspapers relating to the Jewish question with great interest; that is one thing, at least, that makes my heart beat faster, whether in the dreary monotony or in the irritating chopping and changing that make up life here. With Ospel, the civilian in our room, I have a true connection; I am certainly closer to him than [to some of the others], at least in spirit.

I haven't had any more post for a long time … It's the same, though, for many comrades.

I have made friends with Lt. Bitter. I can talk to him about the fortunes of our people. For every single one … the creation of a Jewish state or even a Jewish autonomous region … Whether I'll live to see it, in fact, whether any of us who are alive now will do so, I don't know. Still, many, many of the people we know will emigrate to such a country. Would I? Definitely not! And yet, I don't know whether it might not be the best thing for me if I were to have children: I would [turn them] into Zionists. And so perhaps it will happen that they will m[ove to a] new homeland, and will have to consent to it, even though [it is a] sacrifice, bigger than if one otherwise establishes an existence in a n[ew] country … of course this is also fantasising. Who can know what will happen? We can only know that those of us alive today each have their particular task to fulfil – hard tasks, that our descendants will, I hope, be spared.

It is now about half a year since I was at home and in Bil'che [near Lemberg, to the southwest].

Sketch by unknown artist of Mola di Bari. On the back of the sheet are cartoons and captions, barely legible.

24 March 1919
Postcard
Am feeling cut off from the family as receiving no post. Please telegraph again. Telegrams seem to arrive sooner than letters. The date of our return home is even more uncertain than before. One hopes – April! One fears – September, October! May seems the most likely.

22 April 3pm

A few days ago I received a letter from Uncle Adolf, quite a detailed one! I'm especially pleased that I'm now in contact by post with Uncle Max. I hope that when I get home I'll soon be able to let him know of my intentions. I've already written to him twice from here. As far as going abroad is concerned, I have to seriously curtail my study plan, or complete just some of it, because, if I have already decided to travel to Brazil, then every day that is essential for preparation will otherwise be wasted. The opportunity to educate myself further will surely come my way. And as far as taking leave of my loved ones for a long time is concerned, I think war has been the precedent for that and it surely won't be so difficult when the time comes to leave my loved ones, when here, where I am so far from home, I can do it quite easily.

[Editor's note: Severin exchanged letters with his uncles Max and Adolf in Brazil. Clearly, his own plan to emigrate to Brazil did not come to fruition. However, several relatives, mostly from Severin's uncles' generation, did emigrate to Brazil in the late 19th and early 20th centuries.]

Yesterday, [...] the Easter mass composed by Richard, our former regimental second adjutant, was performed. It seemed to make a pleasant impression on us, and I also believe it is musically very accomplished.

Since 14 days ago, 40 trainee cadets from the vacated Castellano camp have been here, all of whom seem nice, a few especially so, one of whom is Adolf. I have grown really fond of him, to the extent that I can.

A few days ago also, 12 POW officers arrived from Benosk, who had been in captivity a long time, a few even since 1914 (taken prisoner by the Serbs).

The roof has been open since Easter Sunday. We have free time from 8am to 8pm [...] the view from there is often very pretty. The main thing is being able to sunbathe.

[...] probably in return for this privilege, they lock us out of our courtyard with a wire entanglement, a quite strange measure, whose purpose nobody seems to be able to make sense of.

Since Fröhlich went – about 14 days ago – I've started studying more intensively; I've become close to Deutsch, but I've fallen behind a bit. I hope Fröhlich is already back in Vienna and my sweetheart has more accurate information about me from Lt. [name].

'I believe roommates' [wrote Severin much later], Mola di Bari, 1919.
Severin 2nd from right, back row

The new arrivals from the Castellano camp have brought with them a whole library, which consists mainly of consignments sent by the German [Red] Cross. I now have pretty well all the main resources I need for my studies. I'll pursue Portuguese when I get home, which only increases my eagerness for it.

1 May 8.30pm

Last Sunday, a poem appeared in the 'fun corner' of the camp newspaper, entitled 'Riddle', which contained a quite vulgar insult to Jews. It is of course by Kraschischobsky. Thereon a whole host of meetings and resolutions on our part, the convocation of an assembly of representatives, gatherings, agitation throughout the camp. I think that today, Thursday, we have already wasted too much time to be able to appeal to Ferrari with any chance of success. So now the story will have to be circulated, with so and so many pieces of advice and free shots on both sides, as far as is even possible here and as far as we, in our weak minority (18), can ask for.

Necessity has welded us together; if we are of course of markedly different views, then we have arrived at a point where some Jews in POW captivity come to understand that they are Jews by race. It's just a pity that Fröhlich isn't here any more: that would have driven the rest of his supposed Germanness out of him.

The chairman of the choral society has asked Lt. Eisenstein and me, in the name of the society, not to continue to sing in the choir, which we hadn't done since Monday anyway, maybe because we had an inkling of what might happen or maybe it was just coincidence. So, being part of the choral society was a flop. There was a ruse, whereby a few people tried to persuade Eisenstein to go to the rehearsal – just so that they could then 'forbid' him to take part.

Moreover, Wasatsch, according to what I hear, has resigned as leader of the choral society, a consequence that I, knowing the circumstances of the rest, would not have anticipated, although I am quietly pleased about it.

Since yesterday, none of the Jews has attended any course. I hope Klein will continue to run his bookkeeping course. English and singing are dropping out of my study plan. By contrast, mathematics is being added, which I will pursue together with three [others].

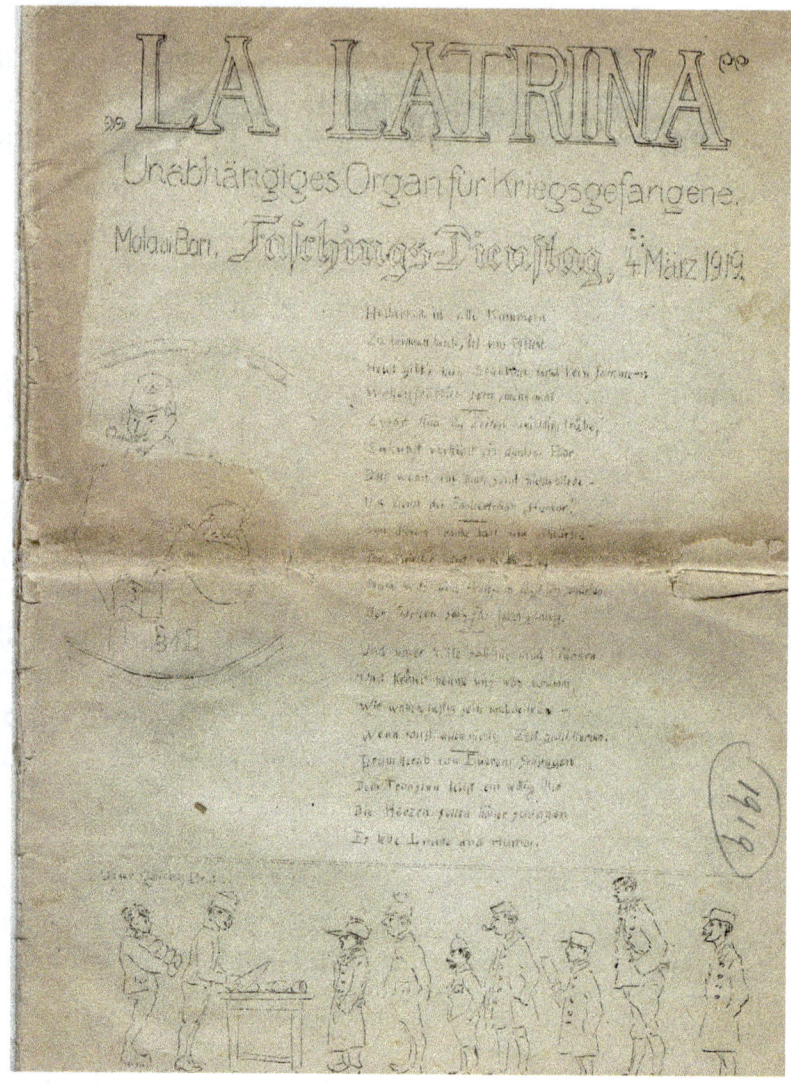

p. 1 of La Latrina
Independent organ for POWs
Fasching [carnival] Fat Tuesday 4 March 1919
The cartoon at the bottom of the page is entitled 'Our daily bread'
The 28-page newsletter contained advice, poems, cartoons, official notices and puzzles.

The Little Gazette, featuring 'How do I become a millionaire?'

FROM BOTH SIDES NOW

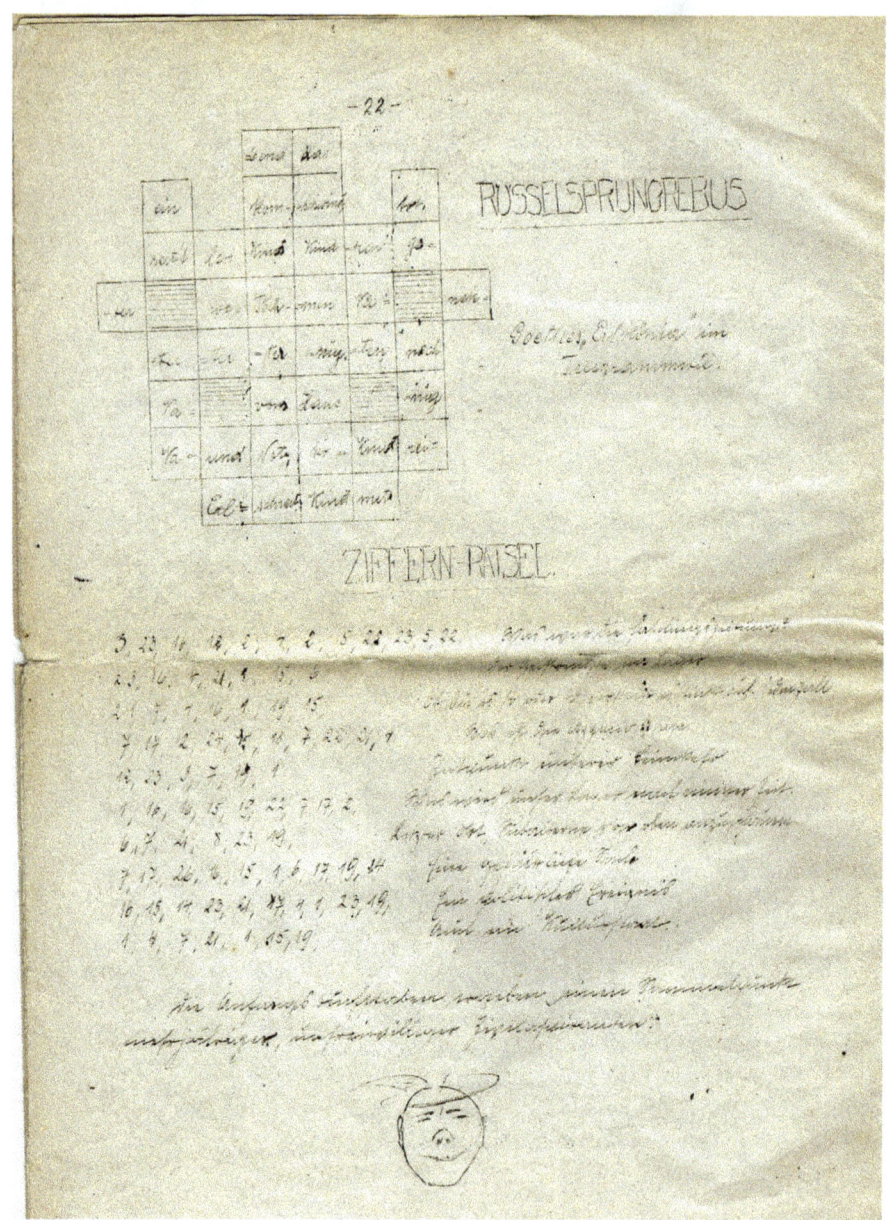

Puzzle page

Above: Three pages from 'La Latrina', the Mola di Bari POW camp newsletter. It was in the 'fun' section of one issue that the vulgar anti-Semitic insult was made

3 May 1919
Postcard to parents
Received a letter from Mama and Walter dated 3 April, i.e. it took a month to arrive. I am not as impatient as you think. The few months that it might take will soon be behind me. I am glad that Franz is making progress. I received your congratulatory telegram three days ago. Are you not hearing anything from Elli?

10 May 1919
Postcard to parents
Events are following hard on each other's heels. Every day brings something new. It would seem from the latest events that we may well be going home soon. For which school is Walter taking an exam? I am very much in favour of the Realschule. There are cherries here already. Immense heat at midday. No news from Elli?

31 May 1919
Letter
I read many papers, but I cannot visualise what things are like in Vienna, whether worse or less bad than we imagine.

Little news in the camp, so I will describe the everyday routine.

There are 13 in our room. The windows are small and admit little air but also fewer flies. We have iron beds like camp beds. There are two tables, fairly big, and a chair for each, plus a washbasin between two. I don't use this: I won't mention why. The plague of flies is often a big nuisance, although the doors are kept closed whenever possible and the windows are covered with organdie. The catering is very good: I am well fed. I eat nearly half a kilo of cherries a day (1kg for 50–60 cents). We can spend time during the day in the outer courtyard or on the roof terrace. We go for a walk nearly every day (swimming in the sea is allowed). Usually this happens between 8.30 and 11am, in three groups (those who go a long distance, those who go a short distance and those who go to the sea). Before that is roll-call, which takes about 10 minutes – all the officers in the camp, of whom there are about 340 at present – are called by name. I go out only very rarely now.

I get up at 6am – or earlier, rather than later; I am usually the first up, am often dressed when most of the others are still asleep. The bathroom is right next to our room. There I have a wash or a shower. Every other day I play housewife, i.e. I take my mattress, pillow, cover and linen outside, beat them, shake them, smack them (I have a lot of practice in this) and leave everything outside to air. Coffee arrives around 6.45/7am. After that, I meet up with a comrade on the roof. We apply ourselves to Italian readings until roll-call. After that, I do my bookkeeping work until 9.30/10am, then Italian. About midday, I do a gallop through the newspapers. Then – far from having a midday nap, whose disadvantages I won't go into here – there's commerce and trade studies, law and Italian revision, in that order. Before dinner there's the bookkeeping course, now shrunk to three participants, but you get more out of it for that reason. At present, we are finishing off American bookkeeping and starting commercial arithmetic. After dinner, there's more Italian reading and finally Italian conversation. As you can see, I apply myself to Italian a lot. Of course, you can't learn to speak it overnight, but I can already make myself understood very well. I believe that this language will one day be very useful to me! Precisely this one!

The days seem to fly by, the weeks pass in a snap of the fingers. Suddenly I will be at home (I know already that I won't be able to understand how it has happened) and will continue to study without a break; for I believe that making haste is even more necessary now than ever. Time presses. If young people are not quick, it will overtake them.

I received two letters and several cards recently, all dated 21–23/2. I hope to God that you are all well, happy and content as I am.

Warmest greetings to dear Grandmother, Aunt Paula, the Molnars and the Steinbergs. In spirit, I fold you in my arms and kiss you countless times, as your loyal son and brother,

Severin

8 June 1pm

Time passes faster here than it has ever done in my life. I study all day without a break, if not always intensively. Only on Sunday do I allow myself some rest; then I just laze about. But I change my study timetable every week, in order to bring some variety into life here. I have received a lot of post lately, especially from Elli, to which I have had the chance to reply at length, as we are now allowed to send one letter a week. Yesterday I got a card, the first since I've been in captivity, from Ida Ruggera.

It's cherry time: we consume vast quantities of them. People have actually got better since the arrival of the new domestic manager, Lt. Dübell, who was only able to take up his post after a fiercely fought 'election campaign'; besides, the election publicity didn't just make personal jibes against Cavalry Captain Läufer, but also a political tendency (bureaucratic Germanness or, what do I know, what to call people whom I don't like) was easy to spot in the whole circus.

13 June 1919
Letter
Many of your letters probably went astray, but I am receiving more post than before, practically every week.

The heat is immense. Washing/showering/swimming in the sea several times a day.

There are rumours, gatherings, predictions. Possible cooperation between Italy and German Austria could secure our release.

News from the Trient girl may reach you before I do.

Dearest Franz! Write more often. I am interested in your impressions and plans. Dolfi [Uncle Adolf] will help you. Telegram me when Walter has done his exam – and for which school? My Lottchen! Please write to your 'captured' brother more often. What are you teaching? How is piano? Are there many concerts in Vienna? I am missing music a lot and will make up for it when I am back in Vienna. That means both of us. Say sorry to Birkenfeld for not writing. I am strictly rationed for letters. Elli will have to go without a letter this time unless I can beg for a card tomorrow.

10,000 kisses.

Your Severin

12 July 1919
Letter

I am unsure what is happening, but I hope that dear Uncle Dolfi is living in Brazil – an enterprise that promises much success, with the possibility of escaping German-Austrian groceries. I have viewed this issue from all sides. I am very sorry not to have been able to see or speak to Uncle, though. The family must have thought I would be in Vienna before Dolfi's departure. Lots of rumours ae flying about and there is scepticism about the news, to the point when people wouldn't believe it even if it were officially confirmed that they would 'depart tomorrow'. I won't believe we are on the way home until I am sitting in the train. Heat and pests have peaked, but we hunt for mice in the evenings sometimes. I am well; my study plan is going OK. Food is very good here, especially the cucumber salad.

The girl from Trient [Ida Ruggera] has written to me four times; I don't make anything of it; the poor unfortunate girl is nebbich meschugge [bonkers]. Pretend that you didn't receive this. I have told her anyway that the post connection between Vienna and Trient is not working. I'd be lying if I said I found the correspondence with her unpleasant; on the contrary, we write in Italian and I gain a lot from that.

Had two cards from Elli. Can't understand why the little ones [brothers and sister] write so little. How did exams, entrance tests go? Has Franzl been accepted in the commercial academy?

31 August 7am

Lately I haven't been studying with as much enthusiasm as before. I have forgotten a lot and am often adrift. Secondly, I have been contaminated by the general restlessness that is afflicting everyone. It has become quieter in the camp now since the Slovakian citizens departed (the day before yesterday). There are only about 200 of us left in one camp. On Wednesday, I did something idiotic and was issued with a quite legitimate punishment, namely five days' arrest and a 15-day ban on going out. I am currently 'serving my sentence', which means I have to stay alone in a room in the courtyard and get food brought to me. Basically, I'm just obliged to stay in my room. On Wednesday, I will move into room 2, where I will be sharing with Lt. Bachrach and Knettler. At the same time, I have decided that the way to kill the remaining time I have to stay here is by studying.

From [Ida] Ruggera I am getting almost too much post. Just as well she doesn't expect me to reply accordingly. At home she is counting the days till I get back. It rather goes without saying that Elli is impatient.

[One of the letters and cards from Ida Ruggera to Severin (nickname Nino), written in a mixture of Italian and German. Ida seems to have regarded Severin as a confidant.]

20 September 1919

Today I received your postcard from the 19th and I am quickly responding to it now. I have kept my promise and am writing to you at 9pm from my study.

Today it's the 24th, it's my 22nd birthday. I remember this date as it's the last time I saw Gino. Nino will say Ida is sad today, and he is right.

It's the same for everyone, but particularly for thoughtful people when we feel sad. It would seem that the soul in such days folds in on itself looking for the saddest memories, sad and painful, does not know and does not want to deal with anything other than what afflicts and torments it. Have you, good Nino, ever felt this despair, this deliberate anguish of pain that is difficult to overcome? I dream of musical chords floating in the silence of sleeping things like a slight appreciation that caresses my soul. They reach me at intervals like poems.

I suffer and I laugh, Nino. I laugh because I no longer wanted to love, I laugh because he has already loved so much. I laugh because I see myself well and I suffer because I see that this is and will be my destiny – always to suffer because I have to tell myself 'you don't see it, that you are born to follow the endless ways and you wait for life, as your life passes by'.

How many times have I already written this phrase. God, I am very sad – it rains every day.

With a fragile soul I cry, Why, oh why have I lived?

That's enough now. I know that once I start I will never stop. Forgive me that my soul is made in this way – full of infinite passion.

I will write again tomorrow.

From Ida [no place named]

Among the Slovaks, none has departed who meant anything much to me, except for Feldbein and First Lt. Gutwillig. Deutsch and First Lt. Klein left a long time ago. Klein is surely already at home.

20 September 5pm
Great excitement in the camp. I have a faint hope of getting out of here by the end of September. Otherwise nothing new here.

[END OF ENTRIES]

24 September 1919
Letter

I 'hope' that the next letter from [the family] will not arrive, i.e. I hope to be on the way home by then. There will be a medical exam for all to make sure everyone is fit to travel. Waiting for transport in the form of carriages from Innsbruck. May still have to wait 10 or more days and they reckon we are going home by mid-October.

The Krone exchange rate is low, 1 lira = 8.50 Kronen; for example, a pair of good silk braces costs 12 lire, i.e. 102 Kronen. Halfway decent durable cloth for suits costs 40–50 lire/metre, i.e. nearly 400 Kronen. But it would not be wise to buy here (and I would have to borrow money from the family if necessary), even though a suit in Vienna, not even one of the best quality, would cost 2,000–2,500 Kronen.

So, you will get Severin back soon. Some youthful escapades belong to the time pre-war; I have obviously developed a bit in the three and a half years, but otherwise am still the same naughty scoundrel.

I would like to expect a nice welcome; ask a housewife to prepare: tea with all the desired extras, the best cocoa, and potatoes without fat.

I have acquired lots of domestic skills, including getting an ink stain out of a tablecloth and mending a hole made by a cigarette!

Please forward this letter to Elli.

[Supplementary pages of Diary 2]

State Law Gazette for the state of Germany-Austria, 1919, 87, [...] 7.
249-251
249 Order of the State Office of the Interior
And [...] 17 April
F. Wegrowski, IV, Radekgasse 5/20.
1. General lectures on political economy, science of finance, economics history and state [...]
2. General lectures on statecraft, administration, social justice
3. Tutorials in both the groups of topics listed under 1 and 2 through the second semester
4. Tutorials in each of the two groups of topics to which the material of the dissertation belongs, through the second semester
5. A four-hour lecture on the more recent history and science [...] to the philosophy faculty
[...] general statecraft – general and German-Austrian state law
[...] administration – administration studies and German-Austrian administration law
Number of lectures missed can be compensated by a choice of lectures on statecraft.
Studies at German and Swiss universities up to four semesters are included.
Main oral exam – 1. Theme of the dissertation. 2. All the subjects covered in the lectures.
Secondary oral exam: one of the three following law subjects:
1. Modern private law based on Roman law
2. German-Austrian or German Civil Code
3. Modern private law on the basis of German law and the law of trade and exchange

Conditions of the order of oral exams
I, II, III, IV
Social economics studies I
Social economics politics II introductory seminar

Science of finance
History of economics
Statistics II introductory seminar II
Statecraft I introductory seminar I
Administration studies introductory seminar
Geography IV hours
History IV hours
Civil Code II
2 seminars

In 5th and 6th semester seminars in one of the two groups of topics.
[…] whether to add an introductory seminar on social economics

Reading list, including books on business, law, economics, bookkeeping, trade, 'chemical technology' and philosophy
Also 'foreign', Italian and Portuguese dictionaries, a pocket atlas, a book on the history of the Jews and several Brazilian/Portuguese phrasebooks and grammar textbooks

Monthly expenditures from December 1919 to July 1920

A list of debts, including to the parents for a spectacle chain

A to-do list for Vienna, including clothing, dental treatment

A list of people to write to from Vienna

A list of people to visit, including Uncle Oscar, Aunt Malvine and her husband Leo (Molnar) and Aunt Fani

Addresses, including wartime comrades such as Moritz Rebensaft, Artur Eisenstein and Dr. Erwin Gutwillig, also of his friend Ida Ruggera in Trento

Preparation for Brazil

Portuguese text book, preferably Langenscheidt
Italian text book, Langenscheidt (Berlitz-School!)
Sauer: Italian

A page of outstanding charges, including lost luggage

Military matters
Main establishment for demobilisation
27.7.19 State Law Gazette 146 Item
One month […] then […] 14 from 19
Medical examination

DIARY 2 ENDS HERE

Letter to Simon (Severin's father) from Tini (Ernestine, Severin's mother) and Lotte (Severin's sister)
Undated
Lotte *writes that she is learning stenography.*
Mother *writes:*
My dear, good Simon!

You can imagine how pleased we are with our golden boy. I have made it my business to offer him pleasant things where possible and he has had a good time. It is a great pity he is not here at the same time as you. The farewell will be painful, but also I am still very happy that he is here with me now.

Today as we were on the tram, Severin, with his usual courtesy, offered his seat to an older lady. She thanked him and sat down. As she got out, she greeted him and said to me, 'God bless your child!'.

I thanked her. I was surprised and touched and just replied 'Amen!'. And I repeat that now again: Gold bless and protect him and send him safe and well back into our arms. If strangers see how good and refined he is, how *could we not love him! He looks well, although quite sunburnt, but that doesn't matter.*

I am eager to have further news from you. I have sent 30 K to your address in Radom.

Otherwise, no news.

I greet and kiss you many thousand times.

Your devoted

Tini

Map of Europe at the end of World War 1, showing the dismemberment of the Austro-Hungarian Empire, the shrunken extent of Germany and the new countries created.
Source: https://www.vox.com/2014/11/13/7148855/40-maps-that-explain-world-war-ii

DIARY 3

Editor's note:
Although this diary was written in 1981, the hand was that of an old man and the shorthand symbols were less precisely drawn and therefore more difficult to decipher than even those in Diary 2. Again, there are gaps, denoted by square brackets. The section of the diary presented here covers 17 to 24 October 1981 and is set in Merano, Italy. Severin departed, with his wife Annette (Anni, here referred to as A), London 7 October, and they were booked to return to London on 28 October.

The last few days of the diary are significant, as they cover the excursion to Vintschgau in search of a beautiful valley of which Severin had heard as a POW and his death a few days later in Merano. In a sense, therefore, these entries 'close the circle' of the story.

Many of the entries are quite banal, although they do reflect Severin's lifelong passion for good coffee, excursions and walking!

beim Fenster sitzen, dann erst einkaufen. abends und nachts ... Schlafe auch ganz gut. A ist den ganzen Tag heiser gewesen.

18.10. zeitig auf und im Wetter. Wie gewöhnlich im Wetter pessimistisch. A wacht auf 6:30 Uhr auf, ist jetzt im Wald, während ich hier meine (Zeit?) putzen möchte. Ich (bin) noch ziemlich belegt in (den) Bronchien. Wetter scheinbar trüber. Es bessert sich aber zusehends.

A führt über Winter... ein Park mit Elisabeth ... vorbei, bis zum Ende, dann über Brücke, schöner Wasserfall, ... über die ganze Länge der O. Huberstraße und über den steilen Weg in 25 (...) Minuten, anstrengend zum Taffeiner Weg, von dort zurück gegen Meran, schöne Ausblicke, Steige hinunten bei Parkirchen(?) zu steil zurück zur anderen leichteren Steige, landen bei Parkichen(?),

A page of Diary 3 with transcription in red type by Jascha-Alexander Koch

THE DIARY
Covers 17 to 24 October 1981
Merano, Italy. Departed, with his wife Annette (Anni, here referred to as A.), London 7 October, booked to return to London on 28 October.

17 October Saturday
… bought singlet and magnifying glass. Schnitzel for dinner. Watched dancing on TV

… sitting by the window, then shopping, in the evening and at night sleeping quite well. A. has been hoarse the whole day.

18 October Sunday
Up early. … As usual a bit gloomy about the weather. A. woke up at 6.30, is now in the wood, while I am trying to make good use of my time here. I still have a fair amount of bronchial congestion. Weather apparently more overcast but is visibly improving.

A. took me to Winter… [?], past Elisabethpark, up to the end of it, then over a bridge, lovely waterfall, along the length of Otto Huber Strasse and along a steep path, in 25 minutes, strenuous, to Tappeinerweg, back from there, towards Merano, [wanted to] climb down to [Parkirchen?], too steep, back to a different less steep path, ended up at [Parkirchen?].

Went into Café André, pleasant, English, only 1,000 [lire] for two coffees. A. went on ahead, I followed. Sleep in the afternoon. … went to Zöschgasse again (as we did yesterday). Nothing on the TV.

19 October Monday
To Tiers [village, c. 15 km east of Bolzano], walk to the end of the village. There had bad filter coffee, went back, had something to eat, all therefore strenuous (for me, with a bag); on the way went by a sculptor's [studio], where A. wanted to buy a little figure, but she left it, as I wasn't enthusiastic about it (figure badly painted).

Bus there 9.30, back 12.10. Not much to eat. A. ordered bread and butter with cheese for the evening. After a nap, to Café Mozart, where we couldn't sit outside (on the opposite bank [of the river]. Expensive, bad coffee. A. found the jacket she was looking for, but not in the right length, with pockets. There was an English-speaking manager.

I went for a walk along via the station, sat in the garden for a while. Library pleasant, surprised by its size, elegance and choice. A. borrowed two books and took out a membership card (complicated). I stayed on and took out a Bassani [Giorgio Bassani, 1916-2000, an Italian novelist, poet, essayist, editor and international intellectual]. Had a sleep in the room about an hour. In the afternoon, A. phoned Bea [their daughter] but couldn't hear well.

A. did some writing in the evening, became very tired. It is a bit too hot in the room.

In the afternoon, A. bought a shawl and a tote bag.

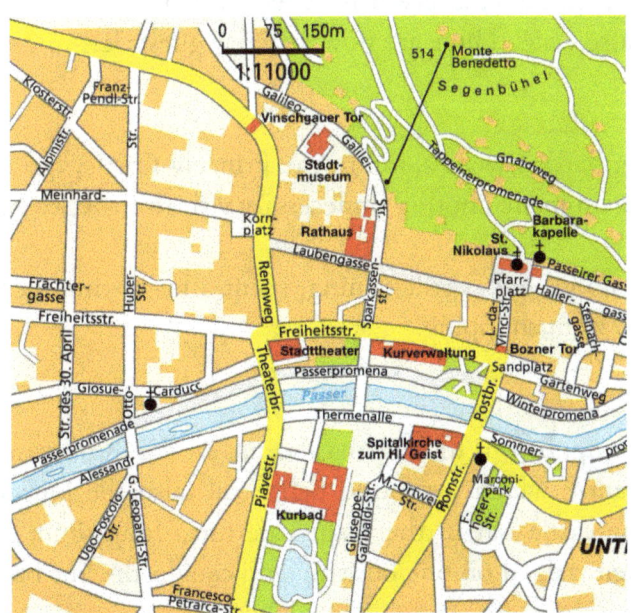

Modern map of central Merano.
Source: http://www.hot-map.com/images/tn/Stadtplan-Meran-7535.jpg

20 October Tuesday
In the morning, I alone to Obermais [part of Merano], back 12.10 by bus. In the afternoon, after a short nap, both by bus 2.30 to Obermais. A. disappointed, went down the steps and on the path along the Passer [the river that flows through Merano], then to the Theatre Café, where we met two people from Basel.

21 October Wednesday
In the night perspired so much that I woke up at 2am and took a bath, then read, then slept again from 3.45. I thought I had a fever in the morning, but I didn't. Mislaid the screw sleeve [? aka collet] of the thermometer, which A. found in my bed.

It is raining. We went first to Sparresselgasse, to a café we knew, then to the library, where I went on the search for newspapers to read. Didn't get home until nearly midday. A. exchanged two books.

We both spent the whole afternoon at home, A. mostly in bed, having a deep sleep, felt better afterwards. Afterwards, I went for a little coffee at the Theatre Café. There are now very few guests left in the café.

22 October Thursday
It is raining hard. I went alone to the Princely Castle, quite nice and old, then again made another unnecessary visit to the City Museum.

In the afternoon, it was still raining, spent a lot of time in the room, although A. went shopping.

23 October Friday
In the morning, by bus to Schenna [Scena, on the southwestern slopes above Merano], which we found delightful (also the journey there). Walk to the castle, sat in the castle café for a long time, i.e. on the terrace. Then walked on one bus stop and caught the bus back.

In the afternoon, had a long sleep and were then rather clueless about

FROM BOTH SIDES NOW

what we should do; not especially good coffee first at 'Ingrid' on the Corso [Via delle Corse].

24 October Saturday

Dorf Tirol [Tirolo, 6 km from Merano] in the morning. But this time took the path to Haselried guesthouse, where we sat outside for a long time, then a little further along the street and back to the bus.

In the afternoon, again rather undecided, but then found Café Aurora on the Promenade, a suitable café, in which I stayed much longer than A. Intend to go tomorrow on my own to Vinschgau. A. phoned Bea after dinner.

The Vinschgau, Vintschgau (German: [ˈfɪn(t)ʃɡaʊ])[1] or Vinschgau Valley[2] (Italian: *Val Venosta* [ˈval veˈnɔsta]; Romansh: *Vnuost* [ˈfnuɔ̯ʃt]; Ladin: *Val Venuest*a; mediaeval toponym: *Finsgowe*) is the upper part of the Adige or Etsch river valley, in the western part of the province of South Tyrol, Italy.

Subdivision

The Vinschgau District (Italian: *Comprensorio della Val Venosta*; German: *Bezirksgemeinschaft Vinschgau*) was established in 1962. The district covers the largest part of the Vinschgau region and its side valleys, in which 13 municipalities cooperate:

District no. 6 is Mals (*Malles Venosta*)

Mals (German pronunciation: [mals]; Italian: *Malles Venosta* [ˈmallez veˈnɔsta]) is a *comune* (municipality) in South Tyrol in northern Italy, located about 70 km (43 mi) northwest of Bolzano, on the border with Switzerland and Austria.

The commune is the northern terminus of the train from Meran<u>o</u>. The trip from Merano takes approximately 1 hour 15 minutes. Trains depart hourly.

This last entry signalled his intention to go to Vinschgau. Apparently he wanted to visit a beautiful valley at the railhead, which he had heard about when he was a POW in Italy. It is not clear whether he found the right valley, but it seems to have been Mals, possibly the Malé that he passed through not long before he was taken prisoner.

The excursion to Vinschgau (by train) exacerbated the congestion in his chest. He caught a 'cold', and on 27 October had heart failure, started foaming at the mouth, was rushed to the hospital in Merano, and died there of pulmonary oedema. When his wife assured him that he would be all right, he replied, in English, 'I doubt it.' These were his last words, the words of a lifelong sceptic and realist, who always needed the evidence before he would believe or commit to something.

The diary entry of 24 October above was almost certainly the last thing he ever wrote.

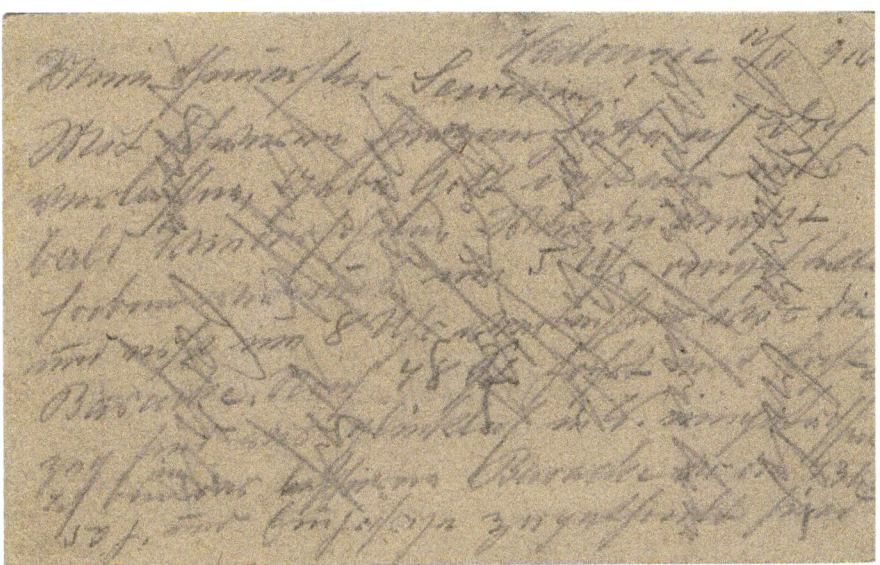

A postcard to Severin from his father, 1916. It was common to make use of the available writing space by writing a section at a right angle to another section.

PLACE NAMES

The following is a list of place names mentioned in the diaries. Some of the names were rendered in the language by which they are known now. Others were given in German, for which the equivalent is given here. Naturally, not only have the names changed but also the places now fall within the borders of countries to which they did not belong or which did not exist in 1917–1920. Severin was fighting for the Austro-Hungarian Empire, which collapsed at the end of WWI. Since then, other changes have taken place, notably the fragmentation into separate countries of Yugoslavia and the collapse of the Soviet Union. It has not been possible to identify some of the places named in the diaries, which are marked with a [?].

From Diary 1 (August to October 1917)

In Slovenia:
Adelsberger Grotte [Postojna]
Assling [Jesenice, c. 60 km NNE of Trieste]
Britof [c. 20 km N of Ljublana, c. 2 km E of Monte Santo]
Čepovan [c. 20 km N of Trieste]
Divazza [Divača, c. 15-20 km ENE of Trieste]
Idria [Idrijca, river]
Isonzo [river, now Soča, Italy, and western Slovenia]
Laibach [Ljubljana]
Mautersdorf [Matenja vas, S of Postojna]
Monte Santo [Monte Santo di Gorizia, Sveta Gora, c. 5 km N of Gorizia]
Peteline [Petelinje]
Podmelec [c. 60 km N of Trieste, just E of Tolmin]
Predmeja [c. 30 km N of Rijeka, 20 km E of Gorizia]
Rakitnik [S of Postojna]
Santa Lucia [Sankt Luzia, Most na Soči, Ladja Lucija, c. 5 km S of Tolmin]
Stein [c. 12 km N of Ljubljana]

Vodice [formerly Woditz, also Kamnik, c. 20 km N of Ljubljana]

In Croatia:
Foglaria [Voglarji, c. 2 km SW of Lokve]
Haidenschaft [Ajdovščina, c. 5 km NE of Lokve]
Lokve [c. 20 km east of Rijeka, 4 km S of Čepovan]
St Peter [?] [Sveti Peter, S of Vodice]

In Poland:
Bielitz [Bielsko-Biała, S of Katowice, Poland]
Dabrowa [Dąbrowa Górnicza, near Katowice]
Ernsdorf [Jaworze, c. 5 km SW of Bielsko-Biała]
Kattowitz [Katowice]

In Ukraine:
Czernowitz [Chernivtsi]
Lemberg [Lviv]

In Romania:
Szatmar-Ne'meti [Satumare]

In Italy:
Boroevič (or Borovič) Gorge
Miramare [c. 7-8 km along coast to the N of Trieste centre]

In Czech Republic:
Heinzendorf [Hynčice, c. 30 km S of Ostrava]
Jägerndorf [Krnov, Silesia]
Reichenberg [Sudetenland; Liberec, c. 80 km NNE of Prague]
Teschen [Český Těšín, about 25 km ESE of Ostrava]

In Austria:
Grinzing [suburb of Vienna]

From Diary 2 (September 1918-September 1919)

In Austria:
Leopoldstadt [a district of Vienna]
Simmering [a suburb of Vienna]

In Italy:
Abasti [?]
Adino [?]
Ala
Barricata
Bozen [Bolzano]
Brenta [?]
Calceranica
Castel San Pietro (Verona)
Fontana Trepale [?]
Frenzela (Val Frenzela)
Gallnoetsch [Caldonazzo]
Grigno
Lake Como
Male
Marcesina
Merla [?Merlo] gorge
Mezzolombardo
Mola [S of Bari]
Monte Chiesa (over 2,000 metres high)
Monte Gargano
Mozzekan [Mozzecane]
Perdin [?]
Pieve Tesino
Pradeschino
Rovereto
San Michele [San Michele all'Adige]
Tollo
Trient [Trento]

Verona
Villafranca
Warlatto [?]

Other:
Lothring [?]
Eimersee [?; near Eckernförde, Germany]
Spilin [?] [where Hungarians were headed]

From Diary 3 (1981)

All Italy:
Dorf Tirol [Tirolo, 6 km from Merano]
Merano
Obermais [part of Merano]
Schenna [Scena, on the SW slopes above Merano]
Tiers [village, c. 15 km E of Bolzano]
Vinschgau [Valley]

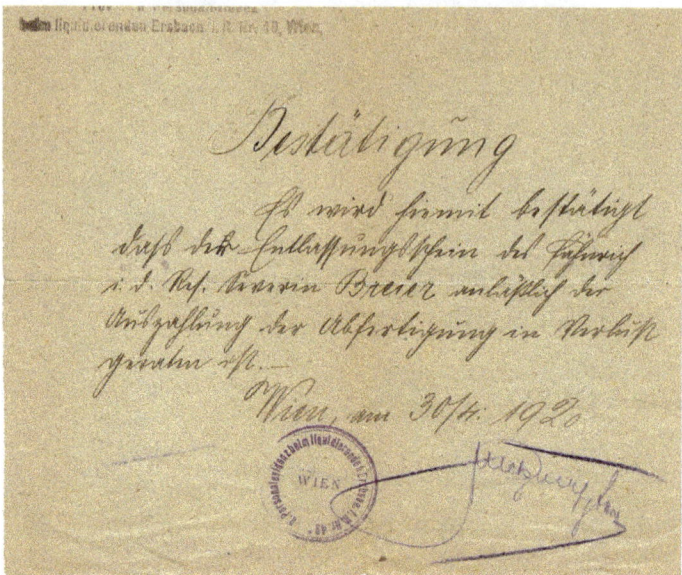

Statement of loss of demobilisation certificate

Confirmation
It is hereby confirmed that the discharge certificate of Ensign in the Reserve Severin Breier during payment and clearance has been lost. Vienna, 30/4/1920

www.ingramcontent.com/pod-product-compliance
Lightning Source LLC
Chambersburg PA
CBHW051827160426
43209CB00033B/1947/J